RAISING
YOUNG ATHLETES

RAISING YOUNG ATHLETES

PARENTING YOUR CHILDREN TO VICTORY IN SPORTS AND LIFE

Jim Taylor, Ph.D.

ROWMAN & LITTLEFIELD
Lanham • Boulder • New York • London

Published by Rowman & Littlefield
An imprint of The Rowman & Littlefield Publishing Group, Inc.
4501 Forbes Boulevard, Suite 200, Lanham, Maryland 20706
www.rowman.com

Unit A, Whitacre Mews, 26-34 Stannary Street, London SE11 4AB

British Library Cataloguing in Publication Information Available

Library of Congress Cataloging-in-Publication Data

Names: Taylor, Jim, 1958– author.
Title: Raising young athletes : parenting your children to victory in sports and life / Jim Taylor.
Description: Lanham, Maryland : Rowman & Littlefield, [2018] | Includes bibliographical references.
Identifiers: LCCN 2018003508 (print) | LCCN 2018018615 (ebook) | ISBN 9781538108123 (electronic) | ISBN 9781538108116 (hardback : alk. paper)
Subjects: LCSH: Sports for children—Psychological aspects. | Parent and child.
Classification: LCC GV709.2 (ebook) | LCC GV709.2 .T39 2018 (print) | DDC 796.083—dc23
LC record available at https://lccn.loc.gov/2018003508

∞™ The paper used in this publication meets the minimum requirements of American National Standard for Information Sciences—Permanence of Paper for Printed Library Materials, ANSI/NISO Z39.48-1992.

Printed in the United States of America

CONTENTS

ACKNOWLEDGMENTS

I want to thank my book assistant, Zachary Vidic, for his unwavering commitment of time and energy in providing the research background that acted as the foundation for *Raising Young Athletes* and the quotes that bring my ideas to life. What is now *Raising Young Athletes* wouldn't have been possible without him.

I also want to express my deepest gratitude to my wife, Sarah, for her love and support in what has been an always exciting, sometimes quixotic, and occasionally stressful journey that is my career.

Finally, I want to express my love and appreciation to my daughters, Catie and Gracie, both competitive athletes, who have allowed me to use them as "research subjects" for my ideas about how to raise young athletes, for the passion, determination, and joy they bring to their athletic efforts, and for helping me be the best sport parent I can be.

INTRODUCTION

Sports can be a truly amazing environment in which to raise children. The benefits they gain from athletic participation are many. Children experience the wonderful benefits of physical health and activity, including exercise, fitness, vitality, and mastery of their bodies. They also learn about themselves as people, including how they think, how they feel, and how they behave and perform in a variety of sport-related settings.

Psychological and emotional areas in which sports help children figure out who they are include their passions, commitment, confidence, focus, discipline, and resilience, just to name a few. From these experiences and the self-knowledge that emerges, sports can play a significant role in how your children develop and who they become as adults. Athletic life can shape their self-identity, self-esteem, and goals, and the future directions their lives take.

Sports also influence children's social development. The opportunities your young athletes are presented with in terms of teammates, coaches, teamwork, and competition against opponents and rival teams can have an immense impact on how they learn to communicate, respond to conflict, and develop relationships as they progress toward adulthood. The mentorships they establish with coaches and the enduring friendships that evolve with teammates can leave a lasting impression on your children. Perhaps most importantly, the relationship you and your children develop through your family's shared athletic experiences can not only leave them with a lifetime of family memories but also provide you and them with the foundation for lifelong connection based on love and common interest.

Sports also resonate deeply with children because they are—or should be—an extension of play, something young human beings and, in fact, all young animals seem to have an innate propensity for. Play is an important training ground for adulthood, whether a bear cub or a child. Play allows young beings to learn, practice, and ingrain essential physical, personal, and social skills in preparation for adulthood. Sports serve the same purpose, just in a more organized setting.

Sports also resonate deeply with children because they can experience a sense of connection and fulfillment that is quite unique from other achievement-oriented activities in which they might participate, for example, school or the performing arts. Mastering new skills, pushing themselves physically, overcoming challenges, sharing the inevitable highs and lows of competition with their teammates, and, yes, winning are just a few of the ways in which the athletic experience can transcend its own rule-bound existence. The satisfaction that can be garnered from your children's deep immersion in sports can be a source of immense meaning that can nourish their bodies, minds, and spirits.

Finally, sports are just plain fun. Sports are, as I just mentioned, just organized play, and children revel in the opportunity to play. The simple act of play, whether running, jumping, throwing (a baseball or football), kicking (a soccer ball), hitting (a tennis or golf ball), or any number of other ways in which children play, touches children in such a pure and unadulterated way that can be readily seen in the smiles and laughter these activities frequently elicit. In sum, sports are a wonderful place to help your children grow into successful, happy, and capable people.

A NEW YOUTH SPORTS LANDSCAPE

But this idyllic view of your children's sports participation is no longer a forgone conclusion in this early part of the 21st century. To the contrary, during the past several decades, there has been a marked change in how children experience sports, that is, in fact, providing them with a very different, and oftentimes unhealthy, athletic experience. This shift can not only prevent your young athletes from gaining the many benefits of sports involvement but also actively inhibit their athletic, personal, and social development, and do actual physical and psychological harm to them.

This change in youth sports was likely a trickle-down effect of the similarly significant changes that occurred at the highest level of sport, including collegiate, professional, and Olympic sports. Due largely to the infusion of television money into sports, athletes can now attain both wealth and fame as never before.

And it is the seductive lure of those riches and celebrity that has twisted youth sports almost beyond recognition.

This new youth sports landscape has created a new type of sport parent, one more concerned with fulfilling their own athletic dreams through their children. This new iteration of sport parents has made competitive results the false god to which they worship, believing early sports success by their children is essential for them to become superstars. How distorted have the perceptions of sport parents become? A 2016 survey reported that 26 percent of parents believed their children would become professional athletes. The actual number is many digits to the right of the decimal point.

The creep of intensity in sports, driven by parents, has moved to younger and younger ages for the kids. It has migrated from the professional level to college to high school to middle school to the various local travel teams for our eight-year-olds. —*Douglas Brunt, best-selling author,* Trophy Son[1]

This zealous pursuit of their children's athletic success by parents has created an entire industry—what I call the "youth-sports industrial complex"—whose purposes are to feed the voracious appetites of those overly invested parents and extract as much money as possible from said parents by youth sports leagues, teams, coaches, and private trainers.

This preoccupation with results at increasingly younger ages has had several powerful effects on young athletes. First, this overemphasis on results on the part of sport parents becomes the central message they send, surpassing the many healthy messages parents should be conveying to their children about their athletic experiences.

Second, because youth sports programs and coaches are fully invested members of the youth-sports industrial complex and depend on their charges' success for their livelihoods, they send these same messages of "You gotta win, baby!" to the young athletes for whom they are responsible and "They will win!" to the athletes' easily seduced parents, which feed their ravenous needs. As a consequence of these intense and unrelenting messages from two powerful forces in their lives, young athletes can't help but internalize this fixation on results, bringing with it expectations and pressure, which, in turn, can lead to fear of failure and debilitating performance anxiety, resulting in a truly aversive sports experience, which concludes with their dropping out of youth sports because it's just not fun anymore.

Third, because of this overinvestment on the part of parents and coaches, young athletes have no real sense of ownership. The adults in their lives are often more into their sports participation than they are. You see these overinvested parents all the time. They are talking about results constantly; comparing their children to their competitors; hiring private coaches; sending their children to summer sports camps; having their children join travel teams; pushing their kids to practice more than the kids want to; and, in general, devoting disproportionate amounts of time, energy, and money to their children's athletic lives. In turn, the overinvested coaches put winning ahead of athletic and personal development and fun, and place additional burdens on their athletes for their own purposes and gains.

Fourth, because the current youth sports culture sends messages to parents that their children must specialize early and play year-round, young athletes place excessive demands on their bodies and minds, resulting in injury, stress, and burn out. As a consequence, what might have been enjoyable and rewarding athletic experiences end almost before they start.

> What we're seeing is that young kids as young as t-ball age are having year-round training.
> —Dr. Lyle Cain, Andrews Sports Medicine and Orthopedic Center[2]

Fifth, these forces act to suck away any fun and love for their sport they might have had when they first started playing. In fact, a well-known statistic involving youth sports is that, between the ages of eight and 13, 70 percent of athletes quit organized sports. The reason: It's no longer fun.

Finally, this accumulation of averse experiences on the part of young athletes creates a "perfect storm" that drains them of any interest and motivation they

> In youth sports no one is losing their job on the win or loss so let's make sure the kids are coming back to play. —Greg Schiano, Ohio State University football coach[3]

used to have for their sport and drives them away from an activity they once loved.

As I have just described, parents today do see the many advantages of sports participation for their children, as evidenced by the high rates of participation in many sports. At the same time, because of this unfortunate shift in the focus and purpose of youth sports in recent decades, you can't be sure athletic involvement will be a positive and healthy experience for your children.

THE BEST OF INTENTIONS

There is no doubt that all parents love their children and want what's best for them as they embark on the journey of youth sports. But let's be realistic, not all parents do what's best for their children. In fact, as we see far too often in the news these days, some parents have fallen victim to the Siren's call of our often-toxic youth sports culture, and their children suffer for it. At the same time, the vast majority of parents have their children's best interests at heart but simply lack the perspective, information, and tools needed to create a nourishing sports experience for their children.

Additionally, it's important to recognize that parents are human beings too and, as a consequence, are just as vulnerable to the messages they get from the current youth sports culture as their children are to the messages they get from their parents and coaches. Parents will inevitably develop their attitudes, base their judgments, and form their opinions about their children's youth sport experience on what they hear most frequently. Not surprisingly, then, when they constantly hear "win, win, win!" from everyone around them, including other parents, coaches, and the internet, they are going to assume that is the right attitude to have.

Also, as human beings, parents are susceptible to the pressures they feel from other parents. Feeling the need to "keep up with the Joneses" and not be viewed as a "bad" parent can further drive them down the bad road of sport parenting. For example, holding their children back from 24/365 involvement in a sport may be in the best interests of their kids and family, but it's difficult to resist the pressure from other parents who are saying such things as, "Your kids will fall behind and never catch up," "Your kids are going to miss out on playing varsity in high school and a college athletic scholarship," and "What? You don't want to give your kids the opportunity to pursue their dreams?"

YOU HAVE THE POWER

In past generations, most of the youth sports culture was healthy and life affirming for children, so parents didn't need to work that hard to ensure their kids had a positive sports experience. But how times have changed. Because of the many forces that can turn your children's athletic experiences from positive to negative, your role in shaping your children's sports participation has never been more vital. Making sure you are on the good road of sport parenting is, without a doubt, the most important influence on your children's sports experience.

Moreover, your involvement in their athletic lives isn't just about whether your children achieve true greatness, or their own personal greatness, as athletes. Rather, assuming the role as your children's sports advocate and actively and positively guiding your children's athletic experience has an impact far beyond the field of play. Shielding your children from the toxic athletic culture prevalent in so much of the youth sports landscape also protects them from the harm that can befall them, for example, fear of failure, expectations, pressure, stress, physical injury, loss of motivation, and low self-esteem, just to name a few forms of harm that will impact your children as athletes and young people. Conversely, everything your kids learn from their healthy participation in sports will serve them well in all aspects of their lives, including their educations, careers, and the many relationships they establish along the way. In sum, when you are a great sport parent, you are also simply a great parent. And what a gift that is for your children.

> You're not developing people for the next level of sports, you're developing people for the next level of life. —*Buck Showalter, Baltimore Orioles manager*[4]

Your goal as sport parents is to provide your young athletes with the most positive sports experience possible. Achieving this objective involves, at the most basic level, ensuring your children's athletic participation is healthy, fun, and rewarding. If it is, they will want to continue, and that is a victory in and of itself. Additionally, at a deeper level, this goal means placing your children in a sports setting that will help them develop the wonderful physical, personal, and social skills that will serve them well as they enter adulthood. That, to be sure, is an even bigger victory. Finally, if you happen to have given your young athletes good genes, if they develop a passion for and a commitment to a sport, and if they are willing to do the hard work and make the necessary sacrifices, they may also experience success in their sport of choice. But this last goal should always be just icing on the cake that you have already made by accomplishing the first two goals.

THE ROAD AHEAD

That's where *Raising Young Athletes* comes in. This book offers you a deep and broad perspective on how to ensure that your children's sports participation fosters nurturing experiences, encourages positive attitudes, and promotes their most healthy development, as both athletes and people, as they move toward adulthood.

Chapter 1 explores the four pillars of athletic success, including values, athletic identity, ownership, and perspective. Chapter 2 considers the five obstacles to athletic success, consisting of overinvestment, perfectionism, fear of failure, emotions, and expectations. Chapter 3 examines your role in your children's athletic lives and how you can maximize the positive impact you can have on them. Chapter 4 shows how the messages your young athletes receive from you and their larger sports world can affect them and how you can send the right messages to them. Chapter 5 concludes *Raising Young Athletes* by providing a list of practical dos and don'ts for you to follow with yourself, other sport parents, coaches, and your children.

Whether your children play sports for "grins and giggles" or aspire to be professional or Olympic athletes, *Raising Young Athletes* can help you guide your children toward their sports participation being a meaningful and deeply fulfilling part of their lives that prepares them, as the subtitle suggests, to be victorious not only in sports but also, more importantly, in the game of life.

> Being a positive sports parent takes intentionality. It's not going to just happen. —*Janis B. Meredith, sport parenting author*[5]

FOUR PILLARS OF ATHLETIC SUCCESS

Your children's athletic experience doesn't begin when they walk onto the field of play. Rather, what they learn before their first practice and before they first throw, kick, run, swim, hit, catch, pass, or what-have-you may actually have a greater impact on the quality of their sports participation than what happens at practice and in competitions.

Chapter 1 explores the Four Pillars of Athletic Success, which act as the foundation for your children's athletic experiences: values, sense of self, ownership, and perspective. The Four Pillars involve the way your young athletes look at and feel about their sports involvement. In turn, they impact how your children behave and perform in their sport. Not surprisingly, the influence of these five areas on your children's athletic lives will be largely determined by how you approach them. If you buy into their healthy aspects, so likely will your young athletes. And when you ingrain these Four Pillars early and deeply into your kids' psyches, you set them up for their athletic experiences to be successful, satisfying, and fun.

VALUES

When you think of sports, values are probably not the first thing that comes to mind. Yet, whether you're aware of it or not, the values you instill in your children about sports have an immense impact on every aspect of their athletic lives. The values you convey to your young athletes act as the lens through which they view the entirety of their sports participation. As a consequence, you should be thoughtful, deliberate, and proactive in instilling in your children the values you believe will lead them to a fulfilling and enjoyable athletic experience, a positive lifelong relationship with sports, and a healthy influence of sports on their personal and social development outside of sports.

> You want your kids to grow with the right culture and values, and the toughest part would be finding out how to instill those values in your kids. —Madhuri Dixit, actor and dancer[1]

Why Are Values Important?

We often think of values as lofty ideals that have little connection to our daily lives. Yet, the values that you hold, in this case, about youth sports, play a vital role in all aspects of your children's athletic experience. You can think of values as a "person's principles and standards of behavior; one's judgment of what is important." As such, the values you have and those your children embrace about their sports participation influence their priorities and goals, and act as road signs in determining the direction their athletic lives take. In other words, the values your children adopt as young athletes will dictate almost every aspect of their sports lives.

Values will influence how your children think about their sports involvement. For example, if you convey the importance of effort and fun over winning, they will focus on those values as they approach competitions. In contrast, if your children believe that you hold such values as winning and being the best above all else, they will think about upcoming competitions in a very different way, likely with expectations and pressures.

In turn, the thinking that arises from the values your young athletes hold will produce particular emotional reactions when they participate in their sport. Continuing the aforementioned examples, knowing that the emphasis is on effort and fun, they will likely experience emotions like excitement and pride as they approach competi-

> Sport can play a big role in teaching values and principles. It can be a huge development tool for life. Just think, teamwork, leadership, work ethic and trust are all part of the game and are also all factors in how we make the most of our lives. —Cal Ripken Jr., Hall of Fame baseball player[2]

tions. Conversely, the values of winning and being the best may produce a very different emotional reaction, one involving worry, doubt, and fear for not living up to those values.

Your kids' values, as filtered through their thinking and emotions, will then have an impact on how they perform in competitions. Again, returning to the previous examples, performances derived from the values of effort and fun will be suffused with full commitment and determination. In contrast, those efforts originating in the values of winning and being the best may be tense, tentative, and disappointing.

In sum, the values that your children live by and express in their sports participation clearly delineate the following statements:

- This is who I am.
- This is what I value.
- This is what I stand for.
- This is what guides my sports participation.
- This is how I will behave.
- This is what I want out of my sports participation.

Where Do Your Children Get Their Sports Values?

As you begin to develop an appreciation for the power of values in your childrens' athletic lives, you also want to gain an understanding of where they might get their values. This awareness is important because, as you will see, not all sources of sports values are healthy, and with this knowledge, you can make a concerted effort to expose your children to only beneficial sources of values.

The most obvious place from which your young athletes get their values about sports is from you. As a general rule, whatever values you possess and express, whether political, religious, social, or, in our case, related to sports, your children are most likely to adopt them. Why? Because they are exposed to your values most frequently, consistently, and intensely from the earliest stages of their lives. Your kids see your values in the words you use, the emotions you express, and the actions you take. As their parent, your children are immersed in your values 24/7.

At the same time, as your children grow older and venture beyond your home, your influence declines and the impact of their expanding world around them grows. This emergence from the "womb" of their parents is realized in many ways, including peers, school, the internet, and, in our case, the athletic world they begin to interact with and become part of as their involvement in sports grows. These wider influences from sports occur at several levels.

At the most immediate level, teammates communicate a set of sports values that may or may not be consistent with your own. As children get older, the influence of their peers increases, and as a result, they are vulnerable to the value messages from their teammates, even those that aren't healthy. Because teammates are so immediate and peer acceptance is so important to young people, your children may have a difficult time resisting messages about sports that aren't in their best interests.

At a higher level, coaches also convey value messages to your young athletes because they set the tone, priorities, and goals of a team and have a "soap box" of authority and respect from which they can "preach" their values about sports. As with peers, those values may or may not be aligned with your own values. As with the influence of teammates, your young athletes may also find it difficult to ignore unhealthy messages from a coach who is in their face almost every day.

At an even higher level, every sports program in which your children participate is imbued with a set of values that are a reflection of its leadership and culture. Those values might range from an emphasis on fun, mastery, and participation to competition, winning, and "survival of the fittest" development. And, as with teammates and coaches, your children will be vulnerable to assimilating the unhealthy values of a team culture in which they are immersed.

At the highest level, the broader sports culture, embodied by professional, Olympic, and college sports, exerts an inordinate influence on young athletes. Due to the idolatry that the world's best athletes are afforded in the media and the desire of developing athletes to emulate their sports heroes, your children may be particularly impressionable to the values expressed by this wider sports culture. Unfortunately, these values, which I will discuss shortly, are generally not admirable nor beneficial to your children's healthy athletic or personal development.

This latter influence on your children's values related to sports is particularly troubling these days for two reasons. First, the money-driven nature of elite sports is now just another form of entertainment that must be marketed and sold. Second, there is the ubiquity of the different forms of media through which the values are channeled, for instance, television, radio, websites, video games, and social media. Considering how connected young people are today, children are easily swayed by the Siren's call of values communicated by the popular sports culture.

Given the impact of values on your children's athletic experiences and the abundance of sources from which your young athletes can be exposed to truly harmful values about sports, it is incumbent upon you to ensure that your children are immersed in and encouraged to adopt values that you know to be healthy and life-affirming.

Healthy and Unhealthy Sports Values

Of course, the $64,000 question in this discussion is, What are healthy and unhealthy sports values? I will admit there can be some disagreement about the answer to this question. Although I might disagree vehemently that winning is a healthy value, given the competitive nature of sports, some might argue convincingly for its recognition as a healthy value. I will also say up front that I'm not here to tell you what values you should teach your children about sports. That decision is up to you based on your overall value system and your specific experiences and beliefs about the purpose of youth sports.

At the same time, I believe there are some values related to youth sports that we can all agree on, and those are the ones I wish to focus on. Other criteria that could be considered in judging whether a sports value is healthy is whether children have control of the fulfillment of the value and whether our society in general would hold a value in high esteem. Additionally, determining what values you want to guide your children as they enter their sports participation should be grounded in what you want your children to get out of their sports participation. Using this measure of the healthiness of a sports value, you can then ask yourself, "Will this value help my children become the athletes and, more importantly, the people I want them to become?" With these criteria as my guide, the following is a list of values I think will serve your children well as they immerse themselves in their athletic lives and leave those youth sports experiences behind them (in no particular order):

- Honesty
- Commitment
- Strong work ethic
- Pursuit of personal excellence
- Love of sport
- Fun
- Respect of self and others
- Sportsmanship
- Humility
- Teamwork
- Patience
- Perseverance
- Resilience
- Best effort
- Embrace failure

- Balance in life
- Physical health

A useful way to introduce your children to the importance of healthy sports values is to also identify unhealthy values in sports and help them see the differences between the positive and negative values. As noted earlier, although opinions may vary on what might be considered healthy and unhealthy values, I believe you can apply the "duck test" to make this determination: "If it looks like a duck, swims like a duck, and quacks like a duck, it's probably a duck." An extension of the duck test might be whether you would like your children to express these values in their athletic lives and their lives outside of sports. Applying the duck test to unhealthy sports values, I would argue that these values meet that test:

- Winning is the ultimate goal
- Win at any cost
- Bravado
- Selfishness
- Machismo
- Demean the opposition
- Pursuit of fame and fortune

Using examples of both healthy and unhealthy values can help you illustrate how these values help or hurt your young athletes, your family, their team, and our society as a whole. You can also really bring the different types of values to light by pointing them out when they arise in the media and using these opportunities to create conversations with your children to help them better understand sports values and guide them in choosing the healthiest values for them.

What Do You Value?

Because parents are the most common source of their children's values, you want to ensure that the values you hold about their sports involvement are, in fact, healthy values you want your children to embrace. The bottom line is you want to be sure the values your children are getting from you are the values you *want* them to get. The first step in helping your children adopt healthy values related to their sport participation is to start with a question: What do you value?

To understand what values you possess, live by, and communicate to your children about their sports experience, you must deconstruct your life within and outside of sports until it is reduced to its most basic values. Here are some additional questions you can ask yourself to better grasp your sports-related values:

- What were the values you were raised with concerning sports?
- What do you value now in your children's sports participation?
- How do you spend your money and time related to sports (because these choices are based on what you value)?
- Will the sports values you've identified bring your children meaning, satisfaction, and enjoyment in their athletic lives?

A difficult aspect of answering the question "What do you value?" involves avoiding clichés and not describing values that have "high social desirability," meaning they make you look good but may not actually reflect what you value or the value messages you're sending to your children. For example, hard work, discipline, responsibility, and commitment are sports values most everyone would say they believe in. Yet, if parents looked carefully at their children's sports participation, another very different set of values might present themselves.

How Children Learn Values

Before you begin to proactively and deliberately convey values to your children about their sports participation, it's important to understand how they learn about values. In doing so, you can figure out the best means of communicating the sports values you want your young athletes to have. You can also be sensitive to how other sources of values can either support or undermine your efforts.

Although there is evidence that children are born with the ability to be moral, children adopt the values that are most present in their lives as communicated by those people, organizations, and cultures they are exposed to most and they perceive as the most influential. The most common sources of sports values for children are parents, peers, coaches, and the sports culture as conveyed through popular media. Teaching your children healthy sport values must start as soon as they begin to participate in sports and be nurtured throughout their youth sports participation.

Early in your children's athletic lives, you have the most frequent and powerful impact on them. You introduce them to sports and share with them those initial athletic experiences, whether tossing a baseball in the backyard, kicking a soccer ball at the local park, or attending college or professional games. Less healthy forces on your children's sports values, for instance, peers and our popular sports culture, don't exert a strong influence on them until they become immersed in a sport by joining an organized sports program or league. If you can instill healthy values in your young athletes when they begin their journey into youth sports, you can reduce the impact of unhealthy forces they will inevitably face as they become more deeply involved in their sports participation during later childhood and adolescence. Conversely, if you don't instill in your children a healthy sports values system before outside influences gain traction in their athletic lives, much like a weakened immune system, they are more vulnerable to being infected with the unhealthy—and highly contagious—values from other influences—peers, coaches, and the broader sports culture.

> If you don't pass your values on to your kids, someone else will.
> —Frank Sonnenberg, business leader and author[3]

Teaching Healthy Sports Values to Your Children

Values are like plants that must be sowed early and attended to regularly for them to grow and flourish. A watchful eye must also be kept for anything that might interfere with their healthy growth. Values must be tended to regularly so they can grow stronger and more resistant to harm. Your children will embrace healthy sports values that grow strong and resilient when the values become woven into the very fabric of their athletic lives.

Healthy sports values begin with you. The value messages you send to your young athletes as they immerse themselves in their early sports experiences become the foundation for the values they will adopt as that athletic experience deepens. The words you use to describe their sports participation should be laden with the values you want your young athletes to absorb, for example, "You gave such a great effort out there!" or "You looked like you were having so much fun today!"

The goals you set for and communicate to your young athletes for their sports involvement send another powerful message to them about your values. When you tell them your goal is for them to have fun, give their best effort, and be great teammates, they see a very different set of values than, say, if your goals are to have them win, in the short term, and make the Olympics, in the long run.

Your emotional reactions to your children's sport participation convey influential messages about values. Emotions are aspects of ourselves that we aren't always aware or in control of. Yet, your children, particularly when they are young, have highly calibrated radars to your emotions, more so even than what you say to them. They can readily and powerfully sense your excitement, elation, and pride, as well as your disappointment, frustration, and anger. How do you feel after your children lose a competition? How do you feel when they win? And are your emotional reactions consistent with the values you want to convey to them? An important focus as your children become more involved in sports is to monitor your emotions and ensure that they are reasonable and appropriate, and that they also send subtle messages that support the values you want your children to adopt about their sports experiences.

The choices you make in terms of the specific sports programs your children join also send a powerful message to them. As you explore the options available to your kids, you want to ensure the values espoused by the sports program you ultimately select support, rather than undermine, the values you want your children to embrace through their athletic experiences. You can learn a lot about a sports program by examining its mission statement, talking to parents of current members, interviewing the coaches, observing practices, and watching games. As you do this "due diligence," you can identify the value messages that are most dominant in the program's culture and decide whether they align with your own. This process is especially important as your children become more involved and decide to strive for higher levels in a sport. These strategies are ways in which you can communicate healthy sports values to your children indirectly.

Talking directly to your young athletes is another effective means of impressing healthy sports values on them. Depending on their age and maturity, you can discuss explicitly the values you want to them gain from their athletic experiences. In these conversations, you can share some of the values you deem important, define them so your children clearly understand the values, and then describe why they are important to you and them. You can offer examples of healthy values to bring them into sharp relief with your kids. You can also engage them in the conversation to see what values they believe are important. This approach can facilitate buy-in by your young athletes because, rather than being told what values to adopt, they are exploring values with you and, in the process, deciding for themselves the values they want to embrace.

As a part of these conversations, you can use the contrasts between healthy and unhealthy as a learning tool for developing healthy values. You can describe to your children unhealthy sports values, for example, win at any cost, arrogance, and selfishness. Popular sports media provides you with a compelling setting for teaching your kids about unhealthy values. Television, radio, and so-cial media are rife with examples of destructive sports values that can bring your discussion to life. You can use these media to highlight healthy and unhealthy values by talking to your children about the media's value messages and how they can impact the athletes and fans who watch them.

Talking to your kids about the consequences of healthy and unhealthy sports values is another way to help children understand the importance of values in their athletic lives. A valuable lesson for them is to learn that if they act in value-driven ways, they will be appreciated and rewarded for it. For example, hard work is rewarded with both improved results and greater satisfaction, and being a good sport following a defeat increases people's respect for them. Con-versely, if they are driven by unhealthy values, the consequences can be severe. Examples of the consequences of unhealthy values might include getting caught cheating or being ostracized by teammates when acting selfishly.

Finally, an unfortunate aspect of having a discussion with your children about sports values is that healthy values aren't always rewarded and unhealthy values are not only often not punished in our sports culture but also actually revered. For example, domestic violence, substance abuse, and the use of illegal performance-enhancing drugs don't prevent talented athletes from continuing to play and be paid exorbitant salaries. Your young athletes will be receiving these contradictory messages almost every day, which makes your job of teach-ing healthy sports values that much more difficult.

SENSE OF SELF

There is nothing more important to your children's overall health and well-being as they advance toward adulthood than the development of a strong sense of self. When I talk about sense of self, I mean the "way children come to think about and view themselves." There are two components to the sense of self that are relevant to your raising young athletes: self-identity and self-esteem. Your children's sports participation can play a vital role in the development of their sense of self and impact both their athletic experiences and the influence of those athletic experiences on their overall development as people.

Athletic Identity

Self-identity is basically the catalog of how your children perceive themselves, both as individuals and in the context of others. It includes their roles (e.g., son/

daughter, athlete, student, friend), personal qualities (e.g., tall, determined, compassionate), and abilities (e.g., intelligent, athletic, studious). These attributes are relatively permanent (e.g., "I am friendly") rather than transient (e.g., "I am hungry"). Self-identity can be summed up in a simple question: Who am I?

Self-identity isn't something your children are born with (although innate influences do shape self-identity), but rather something they develop throughout time based on the accumulation of their experiences and interactions with others. One key aspect of self-identity is that the attributes children come to associate with themselves can be either positive (e.g., "I'm a hard worker") or negative (e.g., "I'm a terrible student"). Another thing about self-identity is there isn't an evaluative component to self-identity (i.e., judgments about how good or bad the attributes are); that's where self-esteem comes in (to be discussed). Instead, self-identity is simply how your children would describe themselves when asked who they are.

Within your children's broader self-identity, which includes all aspects of their "personness," they possess a subset related to sports that is referred to as *athletic identity*. Researchers characterize athletic identity as the extent to which people identify with the role of athlete and its influence on their overall self-identity. Athletic identity affects how young athletes view themselves in the sports context, how much of an impact their sports experiences have on them, and how they react to success and failure in competition. A strong athletic identity has been found to be related to high self-confidence and self-discipline, positive health and fitness habits, and improved performance.

However, there is evidence that an athletic identity that assumes too great a role in a person's overall self-identity can have certain risks. For example, athletes who overidentify with their sports involvement are more likely to struggle following competitive failure, respond negatively to a serious injury, and focus excessively on their athletic life to the neglect of alternative educational and career opportunities.

Clearly, you want your children to develop realistic and positive perceptions of themselves from their sports participation that will result in the development of a healthy athletic identity. The more positive experiences your young athletes have and the fewer aversive and stressful experiences they have in their athletic lives, the more their sports involvement will contribute to a healthy athletic identity. Sports experiences that lead to strong athletic identities include the following:

- Fun
- Inspiration

- Improvement
- Participation in multiple sports
- Achievement of goals
- Teamwork
- Social support
- Unconditional love from parents
- Success

Unfortunately, sports don't always have a healthy impact on young athletes. To the contrary, unhealthy athletic lives can cause children to develop athletic identities that are restrictive and fragile, and not only hurt their sports involvement but also take a toll on their overall personal development. Sports experiences that can lead to weak athletic identities include:

- Not fun
- Unmotivating
- Stressful
- Too early specialization in a sport
- Too early emphasis on winning
- Unrealistic goals
- Expectations from others
- Social pressure
- Burnout
- Injury
- Excessive failure

Also, importantly, you want to ensure their athletic identity is diverse and balanced rather than narrow and too heavily weighted in a few areas. Let me use a metaphor to help you better understand how athletic identity impacts young athletes. Sports are like the stock market. It is risky to invest all of your savings in one or two stocks. The danger, of course, is that those stocks will go south and you'll lose most or all of your money. The same holds true for your children's athletic identity. If their athletic identities are invested in only a few areas of sport, for example, in one sport or only winning, when they don't play well or live up to their expectations, these outcomes threaten their athletic identities. If your children invest all of their athletic identity savings in their sports, particularly just one sport, any losses could be devastating.

Conversely, if you invest your savings in a diversified and balanced portfolio, you may lose some money with some of your investments, but probably not all of it, so the losses will be unfortunate but not ruinous. The same holds true for your children's athletic identities. If they have an athletic identity that includes healthy values and multiple sports, as well as controllable factors, for instance, fun, camaraderie, and effort, failures in sports will certainly be disappointing, but not crippling, because they will have other sources of meaning, satisfaction, and joy in their lives.

Assessing Your Children's Athletic Identity

One way to determine the strength and diversity of your children's athletic identity is to look at their emotional reactions before competitions. Are they really nervous or pretty calm? An athletic identity that is narrowly constructed will feel considerable anxiety because competitive failure will be viewed as a threat to its integrity. In contrast, an athletic identity that has a solid and diverse foundation will be sanguine because the consequences of failure will in no way endanger its stability.

After a competitive failure, how do your children react emotionally? Do they feel disappointed or devastated? Disappointment, although certainly not pleasant, is actually a positive and

> I was very, very shy as a younger girl, just petrified of people. Tennis helped give me an identity and made me feel like somebody.
> —Chris Evert, tennis legend[4]

healthy emotion, indicative of a healthy athletic identity. When your children feel disappointment, it says they care about their sport and it plays a reasonable role in their athletic identities. You know your young athletes are experiencing disappointment when they initially feel sad and dejected but recover quickly and become more motivated than ever.

Devastation, in contrast, reveals an athletic identity that is on shaky ground because your children feel disappointment with the volume turned way up. They feel truly disconsolate and demoralized because their self-identity—who they are—has been threatened by the failure. Their reaction is to lose motivation and give up.

Dangers of Early Specialization

One of the most potentially harmful contributors to an unhealthy athletic identity is early specialization in one sport. The trend toward early specialization in a sport, as early as seven or eight years old, has been growing significantly in the last few decades as stories of professional athletes, for example, Tiger Woods, the Williams sisters, and Olympic gold medal–winning ski racer Mikaela Shiffrin, all of whom were seemingly raised from birth to be superstars, have created the belief that early specialization is necessary and a youth sports culture in which parents not allowing their children to specialize was to doom them to a future of athletic failure and disappointment.

The question of when to specialize torments every parent who wants to support their children's efforts as they pursue their own personal greatness in a sport. Unfortunately, there is no clear answer to this question, but there is some emerging research and the opinions of experts should help you in finding an answer that works best for your young athletes and your family.

In 2016, a new initiative was established by more than three dozen sports organizations, including the USOC, USTA, MLB, NFL, NHL, and NCAA, that argues against the current trend toward early specialization in one sport (as defined as an exclusive commitment to a year-round sport before the age of 12). Research indicates that specialization too early results in an increase in overuse injuries, burnout, and dropout rates, and, surprisingly, a decrease in overall athletic development. Other research describes how multisport participation by children can lead to more well-rounded athletes, greater long-term success, and, just as importantly, lifelong enjoyment of and participation in sports. Additionally, experts argue that early specialization has emotional and family costs as well. An early focus on one sport and an emphasis on winning can create fragile athletic identities, fear of failure, and lower self-esteem. Family dynamics can also suffer. For example, children who feel pressure to win can experience anger and resentment toward their parents, and this can hurt the parent–child relationship.

I should point out that this discussion of the dangers of early specialization isn't relevant for every sport. For instance, there are some sports, for example, women's gymnastics, in which competitors peak before they are 20 years old. These sports require early specialization. Also, sports that are highly technical, for example, tennis, golf, and baseball, do require the acquisition of skills early in athletes' lives; however, early skill development doesn't require early specialization.

At the same time, there is ample evidence that athletes can begin endurance sports, for instance, running, cycling, and triathlon, as late as their early 20s and reach world-class status. As an example, USA Triathlon, the sport's governing body, instituted a postcollegiate development program a few years ago. In this program, they identified and trained recent college graduates who were strong swimmers and runners. The result after just a few years was that the top two women in the world came out of the program, one of whom was Gwen Jorgensen, a 2016 Olympic gold medalist.

Is Early Specialization Really Necessary?

A question I ask myself is whether times really have changed in the last few decades such that an early and intensive start in a sport is now important to later success. Few athletes in any sport specialized at such a young age 20 or more years ago, yet they achieved remarkable levels of performance. There have certainly been advances in conditioning, technique, and equipment that can account for the improvements we see now compared to "back in the day." But is it also due to athletes in the last two decades starting earlier and gaining greater mastery in comparison to previous generations?

One thing that is clear is there is a crucial period between the ages of seven and 12 during which time young bodies are best able to learn and master new skills. This fact raises the question of how much volume do young athletes need during that period to master the fundamentals that will allow them to reach a high level competitively (and avoid injury and burnout). As far as I can tell, there isn't any definitive evidence of what that number is, for example, swings of a bat, club, or racquet, kicks of a ball, or whatever metric is used in other sports.

One bit of information that is potentially telling as we explore this question is that, at least in some sports, early success doesn't guarantee success later in children's athletic lives. For example, fewer than 30 MLB players played in the Little League World Series, and only one went on to become a Hall of Famer. And a 2013 study conducted by the U.S. Ski Team found that success before 15 years old wasn't predictive of who made the national team when the racers matured. What this means is early specialization doesn't appear to give kids a leg up in their athletic development in the long run. A 2015 NCAA study of Division I athletes offered mixed answers to this question. For instance, the majority of female gymnasts and men and women soccer and tennis players specialized in their sport by age 12. In contrast, the majority of football players, men and women lacrosse players, and men and women runners were multiple athletes.

There are also examples of so-called late bloomers who didn't specialize early or show early promise in their sport. They are as follows:

- Tim Duncan (five-time NBA champion) started out as a swimmer and only switched to basketball in high school.
- Alex Morgan (Olympic soccer player) didn't play soccer until she was 13 years old.
- Clay Matthews (Super Bowl champion and six-time NFL Pro Bowl selection) didn't earn a college athletic scholarship until he was a junior.

- Roberta Vinci (professional tennis player) became the oldest woman to reach the top 10 for the first time at age 33.
- Holly Brooks (Nordic skier) qualified for the 2010 Olympics at the age of 27, after only competing in one international competition.
- Christopher Downs earned a spot on the 2008 Olympic boxing team at the age of 32.
- Misty Copeland (professional ballet dancer) didn't start dancing until she was 13 years old.
- Didier Drogba, a soccer player from the Ivory Coast, didn't sign his first professional contract until he was 21 years old.
- Angelique Kerber (professional tennis player), at 28 years of age, became the oldest number-one ranked player in the history of tennis.
- Gwen Jorgensen (Olympic gold medalist) didn't take up triathlon until after graduating from college.

Realistically speaking, I can't think of any in tennis, golf, or gymnastics, which may mean these examples tend to be inspirational exceptions rather than the rule to follow. At the same time, we don't hear about the athletes who didn't specialize until their early teens and, although they didn't reach the pinnacle of their sport, did earn college scholarships or even competed internationally because we don't hear about them in the media. We also don't hear about the many young athletes who followed the same path of early specialization as the superstars and still didn't "make it" because, for example, they lacked the innate talent, lost the motivation to continue, rebelled against the pressure placed on them by their parents, or got injured.

Pressure on Parents

The words of the experts and the evidence from the research are all well and good, and probably consistent with what your mind is rationally telling you. But it's likely wildly out of whack with what the youth sports culture you are living in is telling you and what your heart is screaming at you. Facts and informed opinion may carry weight intellectually, but anecdotal observations, peer pressure from other sport parents, and the messages from our youth sports culture, however skewed they might be, weigh far more emotionally.

If you look at just about any sport these days, the messages are very different than those of the experts. Throughout the country, sports venues are packed daily with kids as young as five years old playing soccer, lacrosse, baseball, football, tennis, golf, basketball, and many other sports. Plus, in so many sports these days, you hear about superstars who were raised almost from day one to be champions: LeBron James, Gabby Douglas, Michael Phelps, and Michelle Wie. These remarkable athletes are in the news constantly, so we are continuously being bombarded with the "If your children don't specialize early, they'll never become superstars" mentality.

Additionally, youth sports are no longer for children and about fun these days. The "youth-sports industrial complex" is big business that caters more to parents with big dreams for their children than what is in the best interests of the children. So, there is an entire industry, comprised of private coaches, after-school sports programs, and summer sports camps, sending the message that early specialization is necessary for young athletes' long-term success.

Truly, the messages we as parents get say if we don't get our kids on the "athletic-success train" early, they will be left behind at the station with no chance of getting on board. And doing this disservice to our children makes us REALLY BAD PARENTS!!

Which Road to Take?

So, which road should you go down? It's a big decision because it could, in theory, determine whether your children become superstars or benchwarmers. It could mean a youth filled with fun participating in many sports or burden caused by injuries or busted dreams. And, it could mean a strong and healthy athletic identity or a fragile and unhealthy athletic identity in your children. Because there is no clear answer to this question, your decision will be more personal, based not on what will ensure your children's future athletic success (because we just don't know how likely that is), but rather your young athlete and your family.

Several questions come to mind as you ponder this decision. First, what do your children want? Let's remember that, as parents, we will be making decisions about our children's lives less and less as they grow. Plus, they are the ones actually practicing and competing, so they should have some say in their athletic lives.

> The sign of great parenting is not the child's behavior. The sign of truly great parenting is the parent's behavior. —*Andy Smithson, psychotherapist and parenting blogger*[5]

I have seen many young athletes who had an unquenchable passion for one sport and were driven to specialize based on sheer love of the sport. In these cases, the parents' responsibility is often to guide their enthusiasm and energy in ways that will sate their burning desire to eat, sleep, and drink their sport, while also ensuring their physical and mental health and well-being in the long term. You can do this by creating athletic and personal balance in your children's lives to ensure their passion doesn't inadvertently turn into injury and burnout.

Second, what is best for your family? Children specializing early in a sport impacts not only them but also your entire family, including you and their siblings. There are three resources that must be considered. First, how do you want your family to spend its time? Early specialization requires an immense family commitment of time, and any use of time involves opportunity costs (time spent doing one thing is time not spent doing other things).

Another resource that is usually in limited supply is money. So, how do you want to spend your hard-earned money (again, except for affluent families, there are significant opportunity costs).

An additional resource that is also limited in parents is energy. Do you want to expend considerable energy in your young athlete's early specialization? This energy can include finding and organizing teams and coaches; traveling to and from practices, competitions, and training camps; maintaining equipment; and volunteering, which is often required in most youth sports. And, as any sport parent knows, there are immense opportunity costs for you personally. These include meeting your own physical, mental, and social needs; maintaining your relationship with your spouse; and fostering other interests you have.

Lastly, what will the impact of early specialization by one child have on your other children? Will the time, money, and energy devoted to one of your children negatively impact the attention you give your other children, as well as the opportunities and experiences they have to succeed (and just live their own lives)? A singular focus on one child can have real implications for siblings and your relationship with them.

One more thought about this oh-so-difficult decision: As I ponder this discussion, I keep returning to one word—values. Ultimately, you must do what is consistent with your family's values. If you value a single-minded focus on one sport at an early age for one or more of your children and are willing to make choices led by that early specialization, more power to you. At the same time, if you don't see the value of early specialization and have other priorities for your children and family, more power to you as well.

Finally, reducing everything that I've shared so far about early specialization, the takeaway is that if you want your kids to stay healthy, stay motivated, and perform better in the long run, the preponderance of expert opinion and the research indicates that multisport participation before adolescence is the way to go.

Create a Balanced Athletic Identity in Your Children

The best way to create a healthy athletic identity in your children is to provide them with values and experiences both within and outside of the athletic arena that foster balance. This notion of balance in children's athletic identity has importance in both their sports participation and their broader self-identity and lives.

A balanced athletic identity can play a valuable role in your children's sports participation at many levels. First, a balanced athletic identity means your children will not place their happiness or well-being on the line every time they compete because they will have a healthy perspective about success and failure in their athletic lives (to be discussed further later in this chapter). Second, they will experience more fun in their sports participation. Third, their athletic experiences will be more motivating, so they will be more likely to want to continue their sports involvement rather than lose interest or experience burnout in their sport. Finally, your children will be more likely to remain healthy and avoid injury.

A balanced athletic identity also has benefits for your children in their lives in general. When sports hold a reasonable place in their overall self-identities, they can better assert a positive influence on the other activities in their lives, including school and friendships. Moreover, a balanced athletic identity won't incur the psychological, emotional, and physical costs an imbalanced one can on other aspects of your children's lives, for instance, stress, unhappiness, or injury.

Balance can best be created in your children's athletic identities in several ways. It begins with establishing in them healthy values related to their sports participation (discussed earlier). Such values as fun, effort, and sportsmanship lay the foundation for an enriching experience your children couldn't find if unhealthy values, for example, winning at all costs and selfishness, lie at the heart of the athletic lives.

Involvement in multiple sports early in your children's athletic lives, rather than specialization, is also a powerful way to instill balance in their athletic identities. By not placing all of their sports eggs in one basket, your young athletes are more likely to find enjoyment in different sports and, because their athletic identity is diversified in several sports, less likely to feel negative, stressed, or devastated when they don't perform as well as they would like in any one

> If someone encourages your child to specialize in a single sport, that person generally does not have your child's best interests in mind. —J. J. Watt, NFL player[6]

sport. Playing more than one sport also creates variety and different types of rewarding experiences, both of which will foster prolonged motivation and engagement, mitigating boredom or burnout.

Another key aspect of a balanced athletic identity involves helping your young athletes set goals about and focus on things they can control, for example, their conditioning, sport training, nutrition, sleep, and effort in competitions. Your children emphasizing controllables makes success for them more attainable and failure more avoidable and far less painful. You can help your children prioritize aspects of their sport that are within their control by identifying those areas and sending supportive messages to them.

Perhaps the most important way to instill in your children a balanced athletic identity is to take the focus off of results and winning in their sports experiences, particularly early in their athletic lives. As you will see throughout *Raising Young Athletes*, this message is an important and persistent one I send to you constantly. In deemphasizing outcomes, I don't mean to diminish their importance in the long run; that's what sports are about for many kids as they climb the competitive ladder. At the same time, establishing an athletic identity in your children that takes the focus off of winning results in immediate and long-term benefits. Your young athletes will have a more positive sports experience in the short run and an increased likelihood of maintaining their desire to stay involved in sports for the long term. Also, as I discuss in more depth in a later chapter, creating a balanced athletic identity that minimizes the importance of winning actually increases their chances of finding success in their sport later in their athletic careers.

Finally, if you consider athletic identity as one slice of your children's overall self-identity "pie," you can also create balance by ensuring that this slice isn't too big and, as a result, doesn't become the dominant influence in their general lives. You do this by helping your children add other slices to their pie, that is, by enabling them to incorporate other enriching activities outside of sport to their self-identity, whether related to school, family, faith, performing arts, public service, hobbies, or other activities your kids might participate in. The more slices of the self-identity pie your children have, the less a negative impact on their athletic identity will have on them.

Self-Esteem

Whereas self-identity involves the perceptions your children hold about themselves, self-esteem involves how they evaluate themselves, either positively or negatively, related to those perceptions. Self-esteem can be seen as your children's overall sense of self-worth or personal value. Additionally, there is an emotional component to self-esteem in which certain feelings are connected to the evaluations, for example, excitement, pride, embarrassment, and shame. Questions often associated with self-esteem include the following:

- Am I a competent person?
- Do I have confidence in my capabilities?
- Do I respect myself?
- Do I feel valued by others?

There are two pairs of contributors to the development of healthy self-esteem: love and security, and competence and control. Love is the foundation of your children's self-esteem. When they feel loved unconditionally, meaning regardless of how they perform or the results they produce, they will come to embrace achievement and focus on achieving their goals. That unconditional love will instill in them that essential sense of confidence and self-worth because they will know that, no matter what happens, your love for them will remain strong. And that love from you will be internalized and become equally resilient self-love.

This feeling of being loved and valued by you instills in your children a sense of security that they can comfortably venture forth into the world and know that you are their safe harbor to which they can return and feel safe. These feelings of love and security act as the foundation for your children's comfort and motivation to pursue their athletic dreams.

From the love and security you give your children comes their desire to challenge themselves, take risks, and explore their limits in broader lives and their sport. And from these experiences they are able to gain a sense of competence and control. Competence in sports comes primarily from your young athletes throwing themselves without reservation into their athletic lives, developing essential skills, and finding success in their efforts. As they accumulate successes and learn from their failures, they develop a sense of competence and gain confidence in their growing capabilities, which creates a virtuous cycle of effort, success, and positive self-esteem.

As your children experience greater success and make the connection between their efforts and their outcomes, they also develop a strong sense of control of their athletic lives. They learn an essential lesson that powers self-esteem, namely, that their actions

> Don't let the noise of others' opinions drown out your own inner voice. — *Steve Jobs, tech visionary*[7]

matter. This perception alone is vital to healthy self-esteem because it causes children to believe that their ability to achieve their goals and experience success is within their control.

Yet, sports are a setting that can be challenging to children's self-esteem. Conditional love from you, that is, your giving of love when they succeed and your withdrawal of love when they don't perform up to your expectations, will cause your children to perceive their sports participation as threatening because your love for them will be on the line every time they compete. And there is nothing more destabilizing and fear provoking than the potential loss of your love. This conditional love causes your children to feel tremendous insecurity, which manifests itself in anxiety before competitions. This fear then squashes their enjoyment of their sport and their motivation to give full effort, keeping them from developing a sense of competence and control. The end result is that you take away any opportunity your young athletes have to gain the many benefits of sports participation, and the athletic experiences they do have produce the exact opposite effect you want, namely, lower self-esteem from their sports involvement.

Self-esteem is absolutely fundamental to your children's development as athletes, but, more importantly, as people. It has been found to be highly related to happiness, well-being, goals, and success, among many other positive outcomes. Self-esteem becomes the wellspring for what your children think about themselves, the emotions they experience about themselves, how they behave toward others, and, in the context of sports, how they perform. One of your essential goals as a sport parent is to create an athletic environment that fosters positive perceptions your children hold about themselves and positive emotions that emerge from their sports experiences.

Warning Signs of Low Self-Esteem

You want to be constantly vigilant about the impact your children's sports participation has on their overall development and, in particular, self-esteem. Of course, as I just mentioned, you want to do everything you can to ensure the athletic environment they are in fosters healthy self-esteem. At the same time, due to many factors in that environment that you are unaware of (e.g., coaches, peers, other parents), unconsciously driven messages that you are sending (e.g., pressure to succeed, failure is bad), or other influences that are out of your control (e.g., inborn temperament), you should have your radar on for warning signs of low self-esteem in your young athletes. These can be as follows:

- Avoids difficult or challenging situations
- Stays in comfort zone and is averse to taking risks
- Experiences debilitating anxiety before competitions
- Gives up easily
- Criticizes self following a poor performance
- Makes excuses and blames others for poor performances
- Performs poorly in competitions compared to training

You will likely see these reactions in your children periodically, as they are a normal part of athletic and personal development. At the same time, if these reactions become the norm and interfere with your kids' ability to enjoy their sport, give their best effort, and achieve their goals, you will want to explore the causes and possible solutions that can alleviate these unhealthy responses to their sports participation. Furthermore, if you do see these warning signs in your children, don't despair. The attitudes, emotions, behaviors, and performances your children express from low self-esteem can be reversed, although, obviously, the sooner you recognize these symptoms, the sooner you can help your children rebuild their self-esteem.

My professional experience in working with thousands of athletes throughout the years suggests that, because you are the greatest influence on your children's sports experiences, if the aforementioned warning signs become persistent and problematic, you should take a long, hard look in the mirror at how you might be contributing to these indications of low self-esteem.

Given the red flags I just described, which you may reluctantly admit to, the immense impact I note may be terrifying for you; you may be thinking, "I'm really screwing up my kid!" At the same time, that power is two sides of the same coin. Yes, you have the power to do awful things to your children. But you also have the power to do absolutely wonderful things for them. So, if you see the warning signs of low self-esteem in your children and the red flags in yourself, don't take them as indictments of your parenting. Rather, see them as calls to action to make changes in yourself and your children's sports experiences that will fundamentally shift their self-esteem in a more positive direction.

> Let's raise children who won't have to recover from their childhoods.
> —Pam Leo, parenting expert and author[8]

From Red Flags to Green-for-Go

Your children's athletic identities can become too big a part of their overall self-identities, which means their successes and failures can have too great an impact on how your kids perceive and evaluate themselves. You can mitigate this unhealthy influence by ensuring that you see your children as people first and athletes second. You can accomplish this in several ways.

First, ensure that your children's sports participation is part of their lives, not the only or excessively large part of their lives. Second, devote considerable attention, time, and energy to aspects of their lives unrelated to their sports, whether school, hobbies, shared family activities, or what have you. Third, be aware of how much you are invested in your kids' sports participation compared to other aspects of their lives. If you are spending an inordinate amount of time, energy, and money on your children's athletic lives, that might be a red flag for the impact that you could have on your children's self-esteem.

Unrealistic Perceptions of Ability

As parents, we all want to believe that our children are the most incredible young people in the world. That perception extends to their athletic ability as well. In fact, a recent survey found that 26 percent of parents believed that their children could become professional or Olympic athletes. But the reality is, that number is many zeroes to the right of the decimal point and only slightly better for earning a college athletic scholarship. The fact is, parents are notoriously bad at judging their children's abilities of any sort, whether academic, athletic, or artistic. Part of these misperceptions come from our desire for them to be the best they can be. Another part is that most parents don't really know what it takes to be great at something (hint: it takes more than just hard work). Still another part is our own egos, in which our children's successes reflect positively on ourselves. The lesson here is to be sure to see your children as athletes for who they are, not who you would like them to be.

Unrealistic Goals

Relatedly, as your children develop as athletes, be sure the goals related to their sports participation that you establish are realistic. Goals that are too high or too low can be harmful to your young athletes. Those that are too high set them up for failure and disappointment—both theirs and yours—and those that are too low may limit how high they achieve. Also, don't impose your goals on your children; that is a recipe for pressure, conflict, and disappointment. Instead, bring them into a conversation in which you work together to determine the goals they will strive for.

Sports Control Your Family

As you have already learned or will soon find out, sports can take control of a family in terms of time, energy, and money, sometimes to the detriment of the family. Your children's sports can take priority in making decisions about your family. This can range from how you spend your money; to where and when your young athletes attend school; to whether, when, and where you go on vacation. Your own sacrifices for your children's sports, as well as those made by siblings who aren't involved in sports, can create resentment and conflict that can hurt your family's relationships. Although sports can play a prominent role in your family's life, to ensure it's also a healthy role, make sure the decisions you as a family make surrounding your kids' sports involvement are grounded in your family's values and the big picture of your family's relationships and functioning.

Micromanagement

Early in your children's athletic lives, you will need to micromanage them because they are simply too young to make their own decisions and do much of what is necessary to practice and compete. Whether maintaining their equipment, packing their gear, getting them to practice, or deciding what competitions to enter, those responsibilities fall on your shoulders. At the same time, as your children get older and gain experience in their sport, you want to increasingly cede those responsibilities to them and shift from micromanaging to managing their athletic lives. This surrendering of their sports commitment to your children sends two important messages. First, it says their sport is theirs, not yours. Second, it relates that they must take full ownership of their efforts and results.

Focus on Results

One of the most damaging things you can do to your young athletes is focus on their results. The message you send, then, is that results are what matters and, by extension, that if your children don't achieve those results, they'll let you down and you'll be disappointed or even angry with them. You also create in your kids expectations that translate into pressure and competitive anxiety. Instead, always focus on the process to the point where you literally never discuss results, and if they do, bring them back to, in the case of success, what enabled them to perform well and, in the case of failure, what they can learn to perform better in the future.

Comparing to Others

Athletes develop at different rates. Some young athletes appear to be "can't-miss" kids at an early age, and others might best be characterized as "can't-make" kids. In both cases, early success or failure has little predictive ability in determining who will "make it" later in their athletic lives. That's why you should never compare your children to other kids in terms of athletic ability or results. If you tell your children they're better than their peers, they may become overconfident and lose motivation to continue to work hard. If you tell them they're worse than their peers, they may feel devalued and unsupported by you, and lose confidence and motivation. Rather than comparing your children to others, always compare them to themselves, specifically, their improvement and the progress they are making toward their goals.

Extreme Emotions

Anyone who has ever been to a youth sports competition, whether a Little League baseball game, a Pop Warner football game, an AYSO soccer game, or what have you, has seen parents who are out of control emotionally. They are either ecstatic beyond reason when their young athletes win or devastated when their children lose. Either of these extreme emotional reactions should tell you that you have lost perspective and are far too invested in your kids' sports participation. With such strong emotions, you are hurting your children, because as they may perceive it, you are placing your happiness on their shoulders every time they walk onto the field of play. One of the greatest gifts you can give your young athletes is your equanimity when you watch them compete. Good or bad, win or lose, you want to be cool, calm, and collected. Your message to them: Sports aren't that important; just go out, have fun, and do your best.

Conditional Love

Let me state this clearly up front: There is nothing more harmful to your children's development as athletes and people, and your relationship with them, than expressing conditional love in their sports participation. Conditional love involves making your love for them dependent on how they perform in their sport and whether they live up to your expectations. More specifically, you lavish them with love, attention, and even gifts when they succeed, and you either withdraw your love or show anger toward them when they lose. It's difficult to admit that you express conditional love to your children because, of course, you love your children no matter how they perform. But that's not always the message you send them.

Remember, kids can't tell the difference between disappointment and disapproval and withdrawal of love. They just see that, "Mommy [Daddy] is really upset because I lost." That perception can create incredible pressure on children to succeed, resulting in pervasive fear of failure, causing debilitating anxiety before competitions and, if they perform poorly, profound hurt after they compete. Another profound gift you can give your young athletes is to, of course, love them no matter how they perform (that's a given). But, more importantly, you should ensure that every message you send them and every message they receive from you before, during, and after competitions, whether obvious or subtle, conscious or unconscious, or conveyed in your words, emotions, and actions, is a simple and clear, "I love you."

> Conditional love is love that is turned off and on. . . . Some parents only show their love after a child has done something that pleases them. . . . Those who are raised on conditional love never really feel loved. —Louise Hart, parenting author[9]

Build Your Children's Self-Esteem

There are no quick or easy ways to build (or rebuild) your children's self-esteem. Rather, it is a process that requires self-understanding, conscious awareness, committed effort, and patience. By changing the messages you send to your children (more on this in chapter 4) and ensuring your children's sports experience supports the development of positive self-esteem, you can create a family and athletic environment in which healthy self-esteem will naturally emerge.

In addition to removing the red flags described earlier, you can take active steps to develop self-esteem in your young athletes. A few simple strategies can get your children on a steady path toward healthy self-esteem.

Sense of Competence

As noted earlier in the chapter, one of the most important, and oftentimes ne-
glected, contributors to self-esteem involves your children developing a strong
sense of competence. You can help them gain this sense of competence in
several ways. First, give them opportunities in which they can gain competence
through good coaching, consistent practice, and success. This direct experience is the most powerful way for children to develop the perception that they
are competent athletes and, by extension, competent young people who have
control of their world.

Second, paradoxically, you can build self-esteem in your young athletes by
allowing them to fail. Yes, you heard me right, failing actually helps children
feel competent because they learn key
lessons from failure, including what
they need to do better, how to respond
positively to failure, and, perhaps most
importantly, that they will be okay if
they fail and can still find success, not
despite, but because of, their failures.

> You can't be afraid to fail. It's the
> only way you succeed—you're not
> gonna succeed all the time, and I
> know that.—*LeBron James, NBA
> basketball player, champion, and
> MVP*[10]

Third, you want to encourage your
children to take appropriate risks that stretch their comfort zone, enable them
to gain more competence, and, ultimately, allow them to find greater success.
When they take reasonable risks (even if they don't always succeed), they get
a shot of "feel good" for challenging themselves, gain confidence in their competence, and become more motivated to push their limits and more vigorously
pursue their goals.

Fourth, one of the most vital principles I hope to communicate in *Raising
Young Athletes* is the importance of focusing on the process of your children's
athletic lives instead of the outcome. This tenet is no less true in helping your
kids develop healthy self-esteem. Good feelings about themselves based on the
process of performance, rather than the results they produce, creates in children
the essential senses of competence, control, and confidence, which grow self-
esteem and prepare young athletes for future success.

Lastly, you can directly impact your children's self-esteem by praising them,
but only if you do so in the right way. Praise is a tricky topic, and most parents
these days use it in a way that actually undermines the very thing they are trying
to accomplish, namely, building self-esteem.

Too much praise of any sort can be unhealthy. Research has found that stu-
dents who were lavished with praise were more cautious in their responses to

questions, had less confidence in their answers, were less persistent in difficult assignments, and were less willing to share their ideas. You can see how this finding would readily apply to youth sports.

Children develop a sense of competence by seeing the consequences of their actions, not by being told about the consequences of their actions. Other research found that children who were praised for their effort showed more interest in learning, demonstrated greater persistence and more enjoyment, attributed their failure to lack of effort (which they believed they could change), and performed well in subsequent achievement activities. Rewarding effort also encouraged them to work harder and seek new challenges.

Based on these findings, you should avoid praising your children about areas over which they have no control. This includes any innate and unalterable ability, for instance, athletic gifts (e.g., "You won because you are so gifted"). You should direct your praise to areas your children can control—effort, attitude, responsibility, commitment, discipline, focus, decision making, compassion, generosity, respect, love, and the list goes on ("You were so focused out there"). You should look at why exactly your children did something well, and instead of saying, "Good job!" praise them in ways that actually help them by specifically highlighting what they did to be successful. For example, "You worked so hard preparing for that match" and "You were a great teammate out there today."

OWNERSHIP

A sense of ownership is another essential pillar of athletic success. Ownership involves the connection your young athletes have with their sport. It means your children believing that their participation in their sports is truly their own—their motivation, their determination, their efforts, their successes and failures, and their rewards. In other words, your children should compete in sports because they want to, not because you want them to.

Children who have ownership of their athletic lives have a great passion for it and play sports because it is important to them and, most basically, because they love it. If you have to tear your children away from, for example, practicing their free-throw shooting or they are constantly bugging you to take them to the soccer field so they can practice their dribbling, passing, and shooting, you know what ownership looks like. Conversely, if you have to force your children to practice, you're looking at young athletes who don't own their athletic lives. You also need to consider why they don't have ownership, for instance, your being too involved in their sports, they don't enjoy it, or they're not experiencing success in their efforts.

> The winners are those who learn to take full responsibility for their actions. The losers are those who blame others for their failures.
> —*Anonymous*[11]

Philosophical and Practical Ownership

There are two levels of ownership related to young athletes: philosophical and practical. Philosophical ownership relates to your children's basic feelings about their involvement in their sports and their reasons for participating. Practical ownership is the expression of the philosophical ownership in their athletic lives.

Philosophical Ownership

Perhaps the thing that most separates children who have philosophical ownership from other children is the kind of satisfaction and enjoyment each one experiences. If your children don't have philosophical ownership, they probably gain most of their validation solely from the *outcome* of their athletic efforts. They likely rely heavily on the outside benefits derived from their participation, for instance, social status, trophies, and attention from you and peers. These children may lack the internal motivation to achieve and are dependent on outside forces to justify their sports participation.

In contrast, if your children have philosophical ownership, you will see that they gain most of their satisfaction and enjoyment from the *process* of their sports participation. They love to practice, take care of their equipment, and enjoy watching the best in their sport on television. Although the external rewards are nice, these children simply love to play sports for the sake of playing sports.

Practical Ownership

Young athletes who have practical ownership are the first to arrive and the last to leave. They put in time and effort beyond the threshold of what is simply "expected" of them, often working on their own outside of practice. Children who have practical ownership often stand out because they are unusually curious about their sport and want to learn as much as they can about it. Children with practical ownership of their sport are hard workers and really focused in their efforts. They are also usually organized and assiduous in their efforts. These young athletes don't need to be reminded to practice or asked whether they did practice. Rather, they regularly ask for additional opportunities to improve, whether to receive private coaching or attend a summer camp in their sport.

Children who have practical ownership are also voracious consumers of their sport, often expressing a fascination for its most esoteric aspects and reveling in its minutiae. An example would be the young baseball player who plays fantasy baseball, follows his local Major League Baseball team closely, knows the stats on his favorite players, and reads about such past baseball greats as Babe Ruth and Jackie Robinson.

Give the Gift of Ownership

Your children's ownership in their athletic lives isn't something they can just take. Rather, it is a gift you give them when the time is right. The reality is that, as I note earlier, parents have to "own" their children when they are young because they're not yet capable of owning themselves. This means making decisions for your children until you deem them ready to make the decisions themselves. This process is also a gradual one in which, as your children mature and show the willingness and ability to take ownership of their sports participation, you cede them increasingly more ownership until you completely hand over the reins to them. The wonderful thing about giving your children the gift of ownership of their athletic lives is that it is a gift that keeps on giving, not only throughout their sports participation, but, more importantly, in other aspects of their lives, including school, relationships, hobbies, and any activity in which they invest themselves.

Philosophical ownership is best developed in your young athletes in the early stages of their sports participation. You can facilitate the development of this type of ownership in several ways. First, as a role model, you can show your children what philosophical ownership looks like. If you live your life with philosophical ownership of the activities in which you participate, for example, by expressing passion and joy for your work or avocations, your children will likely adopt a similar perspective.

More directly, you can encourage your young athletes to develop philosophical ownership by placing greater emphasis on the importance of effort and enjoyment of the process and downplaying the importance of the outcomes. You can nourish philosophical ownership when you assist your children in setting goals related to the activity. If their goals focus on teaching them the relationship between effort and outcome, and the joy and satisfaction gained from the process, they will come to believe that the process is most important. Conversely, if the goals you help your children to set are focused on results, they will get a very different message. For example, if you help your son set a goal of working hard in practice in the weeks leading up to a golf tournament, giving his best effort in the matches, and having fun playing, the message is that preparation, effort, and fun are most essential. If you tell your son his goal should be winning the upcoming golf tournament, the message is that winning is all important. And, because results aren't entirely within young athletes, they will inevitably feel less ownership of their sports participation. Paradoxically, children who don't focus on winning are often the most successful.

You can also encourage ownership of your young athletes' athletic efforts. After they have a great competitive performance, instead of telling them, "You were the best player out there. You are so talented," you might say, "You earned the victory because of your hard work. It must feel really good to see your efforts rewarded."

You can show your children what goes into practical ownership: giving their best effort, putting extra time into their practices, staying focused through competitions, and being organized. Through role modeling and discussion, you can place the focus on these practical aspects of ownership, encourage your child in these steps, point out the satisfaction and pleasure that is gained from this active participation in their sport, and praise them for their practical ownership.

Of course, kids are kids, and there will be times when even young athletes with practical ownership will lose motivation, get distracted, feel bored, or become interested in doing other things. In these situations, for example, if your children have been told by their coaches that they need to practice on their own, you can give them a little nudge of encouragement, ask if you can join them, and even offer a small reward upon completion. If they have time later or another day to fulfill their responsibilities, it can be healthy and rejuvenating to allow them to decide to take a break and go have some fun.

You can also foster ownership by letting your kids be actively involved in important decisions about their athletic lives, for example, what level of participation they want to have in their sport (e.g., recreational, travel team), which team or program to join, and the time they want to commit. As your children gain more experience in their sport and mature more as people, you should relinquish decision making increasingly to them. The more control they feel they have of their sports participation, the greater ownership they will feel in their athletic lives. An additional bonus to being a part of the decision-making process is that their self-esteem will grow because they will feel more competent, more in control, and better about themselves.

Finally, one essential way to instill ownership in your children's athletic lives is to do your "job." Let me explain. In youth sports, there are three important groups of people: athletes, coaches, and parents. Each of these groups has a job to do. The coaches' job is to train their athletes physically, technically, tactically, and mentally to perform their best in competitions. The parents' job is to find the best sports programs for their young athletes, pay the required fees, get the necessary equipment, get their kids to the scheduled practices and competitions, and support and encourage their children's sports participation in the healthiest ways possible. Your children's job is to give their best effort, pay attention to their coaches, and be grateful for the opportunities you give them.

Here's a simple calculus. If everyone does their jobs, your young athletes will take full ownership of their sports participation, have fun, find some degree of success, and gain the wonderful life lessons sports have to offer. But if, as so often happens, you start doing the coaches' jobs or your children's jobs, your children won't have the chance to gain ownership and reap the great benefits of sports involvement. Examples of your infringing on other jobs include coaching your children when you're not their coach (and, especially so, if you've never played or coached the sport), nagging your kids to practice, making important decisions without involving them, and packing and carrying their gear. What a marvelous gift you give your children (and their coaches) when you do your job to the best of your ability and leave them to do their jobs.

PERSPECTIVE

Your young athletes have a limited perspective of themselves and their sports lives because of their lack of experience. They view life narrowly and only into the immediate future. They simply lack the experience to take a long-term perspective on what their sports participation means to them. Particularly with the emergence of the internet as a source of information, your children can be bombarded by the constant slogans, images, or appearances of the pot of gold at the end of the athletic rainbow; they could be the next Olympic champion or earn millions in professional baseball, football, basketball, tennis, or golf. They rarely are able to see what it takes to get there or, as I describe earlier in this chapter, the unlikelihood of such a dream. For example, one study reported that 70 percent of inner-city boys expect to play professional sports when, in reality, the chances are fractions of a percent of reaching such athletic heights. If you also buy into this unrealistic perspective and direct your energy based on this illusion, you are setting your young athletes up for failure and yourself up for disappointment.

For both your sake and that of your children, you should not have them involved in sports unless you have a healthy perspective on their participation. It would be helpful for you to ask yourself the following questions:

- Why do I want my children to play sports?
- What are the potential benefits of their sports participation?
- What are the potential downsides to their playing?
- What are my expectations for their involvement?
- How can I best support their athletic efforts?

Perhaps the simplest and healthiest perspective you can have is summed up as follows: The primary purpose of my children's sports participation is to gain psychological, emotional, social, and physical benefits and life lessons, including, but not limited to, the following:

- Fun
- Love of a sport
- Mastery of athletic skills
- Commitment
- Confidence
- Focus
- Resilience
- Ownership
- Self-discipline
- Leadership
- Teamwork
- Physical benefits of living an active life and an appreciation for health and exercise

It's easy to see how these benefits aren't limited to their athletic lives, but rather will serve them well in all aspects of their young lives, as well as later in their lives. And, importantly, anything else that comes from their sports participation, for example, great success, fame, and fortune, is just icing on the cake.

> Success is not final, failure is not fatal. It is the courage to continue that counts. — *Winston Churchill, English statesman*[12]

Even with the best of intentions, avoiding the allure of athletic greatness for your kids is difficult, particularly given our current youth sports and parenting cultures and the potential payoffs of Olympic or professional stardom these days, or if your young athletes have demonstrated early aptitude or success in a sport. It's easy to be lured into the fantasy of young athletes becoming the next superstars in their sport. Whenever you feel that tug, immediately return to the healthy perspective I provided earlier (you should write it down and place it on your refrigerator until your kids leave for college).

Another part of gaining and maintaining a healthy perspective on your children's sports participation involves reality testing your perceptions of their athletic abilities. Unless you have experience in the sport (i.e., as an elite athlete or coach), you're not in a position to make accurate judgments about your children's abilities or potential in their sport. Further distorting our perceptions about our kids' capabilities is our wish that they are gifted and special, and destined for greatness simply because they are our children. To keep these misperceptions from coloring your judgments and perspective, you should seek out feedback from experts in your children's sports who can reasonably evaluate their skills. A realistic understanding of your children's athletic capabilities will temper your expectations and help you maintain a reasonable perspective.

Also, if your young athletes love their sport and are motivated to become the best they can be, they will reach some level of success and, returning to the perspective I described earlier, gain so much from their athletic lives that will benefit them well in the future. As I told the parent of one young athlete with limited athletic ability but immense drive and commitment, "Your son may not become that successful in his sport, but he will become successful at *something*."

As I mention earlier, predicting future success is an uncertain endeavor. Think of all the "can't-miss kids" who missed. And think of the ones who just "didn't have what it takes," yet somehow they achieved athletic greatness anyway. An assessment of your children's capabilities should not be used to determine how much support and encouragement you give them. And it should never be used to set limits on your children's dreams and goals. To paraphrase Confucius, "If you don't aim for the stars, you will never even reach the moon." Rather, whatever ability your young athletes appear to have now, no one really knows how good they can be in the future. So, you should simply focus on what you can do to support your children's goals and efforts. Only then will they not just gain the wonderful benefits of sports participation but also make it as far as their talent and efforts will take them.

You can further reinforce this healthy perspective and withstand the forces you will certainly feel from our youth sports culture by making one simple assumption: that your children will not become sports superstars. Paradoxically, by going on this assumption, if you gave them great athletic genes, if they have a passion for their sport, if they are willing to work hard, if they are able to stay focused on their athletic dreams, and if they are lucky enough to avoid injuries, this "no superstar" assumption on your part will actually increase the chances of their dream of athletic greatness coming true (and, if not, getting as far as they can in their sport) because they will feel no pressure from you to become superstars.

Perhaps the most important role you can play with your children is to offer them different perspectives on their sports experiences. As noted earlier in this chapter, your children have limited ability to consider different ways of looking at themselves and their world. Because of their lack of experience, lack of cognitive sophistication, and emotional vulnerability, they will accept the perspective that is most powerfully evident and immediately attractive to them. When, for example, they are surrounded by kids who talk constantly about winning, it is extremely difficult for them to resist these "It's all about results" messages from their peers. The values and attitudes that underlie these messages will seep into your children's brains without them realizing it and likely become their own, unless you provide them with another perspective.

It is your responsibility to offer your young athletes another point of view that will keep them from absorbing the harmful messages of the youth sports culture. This perspective begins with you being a "critical" parent. When I say critical, I don't mean critical of your children. Rather, I mean you need to look critically at the many aspects of the youth sports culture your children are exposed to, judge what messages they might be getting, and provide healthy perspectives that will mitigate the negative messages and highlight the many positive messages they can get from their sports participation. In offering different perspectives to your children, they learn to view their athletic experiences through a healthy lens that will benefit them as both athletes and young people rather than through the lens of the current youth sports culture.

> Success comes from knowing that you did your best to become the best you are capable of becoming. —*John Wooden, legendary college basketball coach*[13]

FIVE OBSTACLES TO
ATHLETIC SUCCESS

In my decades of working with young athletes, I have seen many who were physically gifted, hardworking, and intelligent. They seemed to be destined for success in their sport. Yet, these athletes consistently underperformed and never realized the potential they exhibited early in their sports lives. These apparent failures were a cause of some consternation to me early in my career in sport psychology; "What prevented them from performing up to their obvious capabilities?" I asked myself.

It wasn't until I began to explore the role of the mind more deeply and work closely with the parents of athletes that I was able to answer that question. In my professional development, I started to plumb the depths of the athletic psyche and connect the dots between athletes and their parents. In doing so, issues that aren't normally addressed in mental training, yet have an immense impact on young athletes, emerged that offer a rich explanation for why these supposedly "can't-miss" kids did, in fact, miss.

From these explorations, I've identified five "obstacles" that can block young athletes' path to their goals and, not surprisingly, are significantly influenced—either positively or negatively—by parents:

- Overinvestment
- Perfectionism
- Fear of failure
- Emotions
- Expectations

These obstacles are actually attitudes that young athletes developed both within and outside of sports. Paradoxically, these attitudes start out not as obstacles at all, but, early in their sports participation, actually propelled them toward success on the field of play. They created a single-minded focus, an unwillingness to accept anything less than the best, a powerful need to avoid failure, a strong desire to avoid painful emotions, and extremely high standards.

However, at some point, these athletes' psychological and emotional winds shifted from a wind at their back pushing them forward to a headwind that slowed them down. What had once been attitudes that drove success became obstacles that made success nearly impossible to achieve. Moreover, these obstacles create a lose–lose situation in which these athletes are not only unable to perform up to their capabilities and achieve their goals, but also their sports participation is a truly aversive experience (e.g., stressful, no fun, negative feelings) that drives them from their sport.

> Obstacles are those frightful things you see when you take your eyes off your goal. — Henry Ford, automotive pioneer[1]

Chapter 2 examines several key aspects of these obstacles:

- How these obstacles develop
- Who or what causes them
- How they impact young athletes psychologically, emotionally, athletically, and personally
- What the consequences are of these harmful attitudes on young athletes
- How parents can help their children tear down these obstacles and replace them with healthy attitudes to support their athletic efforts

OVERINVESTMENT

The investment you make in your young athletes' sports participation is another wonderful gift you can give them. The time, money, energy, resources, and love you give to their athletic pursuits send a powerful message about your commitment to their sports involvement. But there is a fine line between investing and overinvesting in your children's athletic lives. And the consequences of how much you invest in your kids' sports participation will be either positive or negative, but, in either case, they will be substantial.

When you make a healthy investment in your young athletes, they will feel motivated and confident. Your children will be calm, focused on performing their best, and having fun when they enter the field of play. Their sports experiences will be inspiring, gratifying, and a source of great satisfaction. And your kids will gain the amazing benefits that should be the primary reason why you have them in sports in the first place.

In contrast, when you become overly invested in your young athletes' lives, they have a diametrically opposed sports experience. They see their involvement through a decidedly negative lens of doubt, worry, and anxiety. Your children will focus on results to their detriment; they will feel pressure to win and scared to lose. Because they know that you've invested so much, they will be afraid of letting you down and causing you to feel that your investment wasn't worth it. And, because of this burden, your children not only fail to gain the essential benefits of sports, but also, sadly, their athletic involvement becomes unpleasant and these unpleasant experiences suck the fun out of and drive them away from sports.

"Too" Zone

As a sports parent, you obviously care about your children's athletic lives. If you didn't see value in sports, you wouldn't have them playing in the first place. But you know that you're overinvested in their sports participation when you enter what I call the "too" zone. Doing anything *too* is not a good thing, whether eating too much ice cream, working too hard, or caring too much about your children's sports involvement. In fact, *too* is one of the most dangerous words in sport parenting. It occurs when you invest too much of your self-identity and self-esteem—how you view and feel about yourself as a person and a parent—in your children's sports participation.

> Overthinking is just a painful reminder that you care way too much, even when you shouldn't.
> —*Anonymous*[2]

You want to care about your kids' sports, but you don't want to care too much. You want their sports to be important to you, but you don't want it to be too important. You want to support your children's efforts, but you don't want to support them too much and for the wrong reasons. Contrary to your good intentions, your reactions to your kids' athletic efforts when you are in the too zone aren't positive, pleasant, or supportive of their sports experiences. And they can quickly turn their sports participation from great to bad to worse.

Overinvestment and Emotions

Your emotions before, during, and after a competition are a good metric of your investment in your children's athletic lives. Here's a good analogy. You hear about what seems like a great financial opportunity from a friend with a potentially big payout. You have two options. Play it safe and only invest a small amount or take a risk and invest a large amount. As the investment opportunity reaches its payoff, what will your emotional reactions be before and after the announcement based on the two levels of investment? Before, you'll feel a bit nervous because you might incur a small loss or in a state of profound trepidation because you have so much on the line. Afterward, if the investment pays off, you'll feel excited about the small investment or relieved about the big investment. If it doesn't pay off, you'll feel either some disappointment or absolute devastation.

Now, let's return to the investment you make in children's sports participation. Before competitions, are you relaxed and carefree or stressed and worried? During games, are you a mostly dispassionate observer enjoying seeing your children play or a rabid fan who is living and dying on every play? After the event, are you just proud of your children's participation, regardless of the outcome, or are you either ecstatic in victory or disconsolate in defeat?

> When little people are overwhelmed by big emotions, it's our job to share our calm, not join their chaos. —L. R. Knost, author and child development researcher[3]

"We" Syndrome

One of the biggest red flags I see with parents when they become overly invested in their children's sports participation is when they suffer from what I call the "we" syndrome. In other words, this is when they say things like, "We better get out there and practice for the game this weekend," "We're going to win today!" or "We beat them!" Correct me if I'm wrong, but parents don't actually practice or perform in the competitions, the kids do. You might think saying "we" is just a natural part of being the parents of young athletes and that you don't really mean "we." Well, you may not mean "we," but that's what you say and that's what your kids hear.

When you say "we" or "our," you are taking away your children's ability to say "I" or "mine." In other words, you are taking away their ownership of their sports participation and communicating to them that their athletic lives are yours as much as theirs, saying it is "our" thing instead of "their" thing. Furthermore, as I discussed in chapter 1, without full ownership of their sports involvement, your children won't put all they can into their sport, and they won't get all they can out of their sport. The cure for the "we" syndrome is simple. Be sure that when you talk to your kids about their sport, you never say "we" and, in doing so, make it clear that their sports participation is theirs, not yours, and that you are there to support their efforts and goals.

What ROI Are You Looking For?

Let's be realistic. As parents, we all want to see our investment in our children pay off. In the financial world, that payoff is called "return on investment," or ROI. There is a big difference in the ROI that parents are looking for when they have a healthy as compared to an excessive investment in their young athletes. For those parents with a healthy investment, the only ROIs they are looking for are fun, love of sports, an appreciation for health and fitness, and those important life lessons and skills that will serve their children well throughout their lives.

By contrast, parents who have become overly invested in their children's athletic lives shift away from ROIs that are healthy and likely embrace ROIs based on results, fame, and fortune, all of which are often harmful and, in reality, a near-statistical impossibility. In other words, overinvested parents are looking for payoffs in terms of victories, wealth, and celebrity for their young athletes and, by extension, themselves (think Richard Williams, father of Venus and Serena, and LaVar Ball, father of Lonzo), and financial reward for themselves.

At a deeper level, sports parents who become overly invested in their children's athletic experiences base their self-esteem on how their kids perform and the results they produce. Thus, every competition is a potential threat to these parents' view of themselves, and their young athletes feel immense pressure to not let their parents down. Some athletes, admittedly, rise to the occasion, and their parents receive a huge ROI. But far more crumble under this weight, and the ROI is zero or negative in every way.

You want to ask yourself two questions. First, what kind of ROI are you looking for from your kid's sports participation? If it is grounded in the healthy values described in chapter 1—fun, physical health, and essential life skills gained from sports—your investment is reasonable and will likely be rewarded; however, if your investment is more closely tied to results and your own needs and goals, you'll want to do the following:

- Reevaluate your investment.
- Consider the unlikelihood of receiving a ROI on your investment.

- Recognize that you are actually hurting your children.
- Seriously consider making a change in your investment "strategy" with your young athletes.

Second, how invested are you in your children's sports participation? If you find yourself saying, "Oh my gosh, that's me!" to my descriptions of the "too" zone and your emotions, you are probably overly invested in their athletic lives and may want to examine a few key areas:

- Why are you overly invested in your young athletes?
- What unhealthy needs of yours are being met?
- How can you reduce your investment to a healthy level?

Three Words to Live By

One of the most impactful recommendations I can give you and one of the greatest gifts you can give your young athletes if you come to realize you are overly invested in your children's athletic lives can be expressed in three simple, yet powerful, words: *GET A LIFE!* At the core of parents being overly invested in their kids' sports participation is that they don't have a life of their own that meets their own needs. Their lives don't provide them with the meaning, satisfaction, and validation that will leave them happy and fulfilled without placing that burden on their children's shoulders. Having a life of your own, whether marriage, career, avocations, or friends, that offers you those "warm fuzzies" allows your children to have their own lives, both on and off the field of play.

PERFECTIONISM

As parents, part of us wants to have perfect children. They get straight As in school; are star athletes; are perfectly well mannered, kind, and considerate; and are universally loved by adults and peers alike. Wouldn't that make life as a parent so much easier and more gratifying? At the same time, there is an ugly side to so-called perfect children. Research has shown they are often insecure, fearful, and constantly stressed. These perfect children are also self-critical, pleasers, and never satisfied with their efforts. Perfectionism is linked to debilitating anxiety and depression, and may also be a risk factor for eating disorders, substance abuse, and suicide.

Interestingly, although perfectionists usually reach a high level of success (because they push themselves unmercifully), they often never quite make it to the top because their impossibly high standards create fear of failure, crippling anxiety, doubt, and risk aversion. In fact, the people who reach the top of their fields are actually more likely to reject perfectionism because they learn that taking risks, making mistakes, and experiencing failure are vitally important to the pursuit of greatness. Quite simply, perfectionists are often unhappy because they are constantly faced with the reality that they will never be perfect. In sum, although perfect children sound good on paper, perfection in your children is the last thing you would want for or expect from them.

Understanding Perfectionism in Your Young Athletes

You know you have perfectionistic young athletes when they set impossibly high standards for themselves and pursue goals that are, for all intents and purposes, unattainable. When perfectionistic children inevitably fail to meet those unreasonably high standards, they punish themselves with self-criticism for not being perfect. You can identify perfectionism in your children when they are never satisfied with their efforts no matter how objectively well they perform. For example, after I spoke to a group of athletes recently, a girl from the audience described to me how she had won her last two tennis tournaments. Yet, the fact that she lost three sets during her string of victories had been eating her alive ever since.

At the heart of perfectionism lies a threat: If children aren't perfect, something bad will happen. The most common bad things that perfectionists fear include the following thoughts:

- "I will be a worthless person."
- "My parents won't love me."
- "My friends won't like me."
- "Everyone will think I'm a loser."
- "I'll fail at everything I do."

This threat arises because young athletes connect whether they are perfect with their self-esteem (see chapter 1); being perfect dictates whether they see themselves as valuable people worthy of love and respect. The price these children believe they will pay if they are not perfect is immense, both athletically and personally, and its toll can be, as noted earlier, truly destructive.

By the way, young athletes don't have to be perfectionistic in every part of their lives to be considered perfectionists. They only have to be perfect in areas they care about, for example, there are perfectionistic athletes whose rooms are pigsties or who don't care about how they do in school.

Perfectionists Abhor Failure

In all likelihood, when you see perfectionism in your young athletes you will also see fear of failure (to be discussed in the next section). Although perfectionistic children give the impression they are pursuing success with great determination, the sad reality is their primary motivation in sports and, often, other aspects of their lives is to simply avoid failure because failure is the most extreme form of imperfection. Imagine your perfectionistic young athletes being chased relentlessly by a mountain lion—if it catches them, they will be eaten—and you can get a sense of what being imperfect means to them.

Perfectionists Struggle with Emotions

The emotions your young athletes experience in their sports efforts are a major "tell" about how perfectionistic they are because the emotional lives of perfectionists related to their sports participation are neither healthy nor pleasant. There are several emotional reactions that separate healthy striving for athletic success from unhealthy need for athletic success.

Most athletes when they perform well and achieve their competitive goals feel such wonderful emotions as elation, excitement, joy, and pride. But perfectionistic young athletes rarely feel these positive emotions. Instead, a red flag should go up for you when you see your children experiencing relief after having found some success. Where does this relief come from? They once again avoided true imperfection and can continue to feel okay about themselves for a little while longer. But that relief is short-lived. Recently, I asked a group of perfectionistic young athletes how long they thought the relief lasts, and one boy threw up his hand and declared, "Till the game!"

In response to failure in their sport, most young athletes would naturally feel disappointment, which, although unpleasant, is a positive emotion because it acts to motivate them to continue to pursue success so as to avoid disappointment in the future. By contrast, if you have a perfectionistic athlete, you will likely see a painful concoction of devastation, with equal parts dejection, hurt, humiliation, shame, anger, and frustration, which is not only incredibly unpleasant for your children to experience, but also it acts to demotivate them and removes their enjoyment from their sports experiences.

Where Do Your Children Get Their Perfectionism?

One of the most frequent comments I get from parents of perfectionistic athletes is, "I swear that my child was born a perfectionist." While believing this explanation may reduce parents' guilt about their children's perfectionism, there is no scientific evidence that it is an inherited trait. To the contrary, the research indicates children learn their perfectionism from their parents, most often from their same-sex parent. There may, however, be an indirect genetic influence. Temperament, which is inborn, may make children more vulnerable to perfectionism. For example, some children are born more emotionally sensitive and, as a result, would be more aware of the subtle messages from their perfectionistic parents, making them more likely to internalize those messages of perfectionism.

Are you a perfectionist? If so, you can pass on your perfectionism to your young athletes in three ways. You can actively reward success and punish failure. For example, you could offer or withdraw your love based on whether your children meet your perfectionistic expectations. When your children succeed, you might lavish them with love, attention, and gifts. But when they fail, you might either withdraw your love and become cold and distant, or express strong anger and resentment toward your children. In both cases, your children would get the message that if they want your love, they must be perfect. Thankfully, in my decades working with sport families, I have only come across a few parents who were this overtly perfectionistic.

You can also unintentionally encourage perfectionism in your children by modeling perfectionism. Examples of how you might indirectly send messages of perfectionism include always needing to look a certain way, the effort you put into your professional life, your competitiveness in sports and games, and how you respond when things don't go your way. In these cases, your young athletes see how tough you are on yourself when you're not perfect, so they come to feel that they must also be perfect. You unwittingly communicate to your children that anything less than perfection won't be tolerated in your family.

The final way you can create perfectionistic young athletes is to project your flaws onto your children and try to fix those flaws in them by expecting them to be flawless. Unfortunately, instead of creating perfect children and absolving yourself of your own imperfections, you pass them on to your children and stay flawed yourself.

Raise Excellent Children

Just as you have the power to raise perfectionistic young athletes, you can also wield that same influence to raise them to be simply excellent young athletes and people, a goal that makes them not only more successful but also far happier. In fact, excellence is my antidote to the burden of perfectionism. You should start by removing the word *perfection* from your vocabulary. Most of the time that you use the word *perfect*, you probably don't mean it in the literal sense, for example, "It was a perfect day" or "You are perfect." But kids are literal beings; they think what you say communicates what is important to you. Every time you use perfect and your children hear perfect, it's a constant reminder to them that they need to be perfect. In sum, using the word perfect serves no purpose other than to instill in them a belief that they must be perfect, which, ultimately, will make your children miserable.

Your best antidote to this malady is to inspire your children to strive for excellence. Excellence draws on the positive aspects of perfection (e.g., striving for goals, setting high standards) but removes its unhealthy parts (e.g., connecting results with self-esteem, unrealistic expectations, fear of failure). Excellence still holds your young athletes to a high standard—it's not above average, good, or very good, it's excellent—and encourages them to be the best athletes they can be, but it relieves them of the burden of *needing* to be perfect to feel loved, valued, and accepted by you, their social world, or, even worse, themselves. Without the fear of failure that coexists with perfectionism, your children can turn their gaze toward athletic success, accept the inevitable mistakes and failures, and pursue their goals with commitment and gusto, knowing that, win or lose, you will always love them and they will be okay. The result is that they are actually more likely to find the success they strive for, and they will enjoy the experience far more.

> Striving for excellence feels wonderful because you're trying your very best. Perfectionism feels terrible because your work is somehow never quite good enough. —*Anonymous*[4]

If you are a perfectionist, one of the great gifts you can give your children is to recognize and reject your own perfectionism. If you don't make what will certainly be a Herculean effort, you will likely pass on your perfectionism to them. And that is definitely not a burden you want them to take on.

I also encourage you to be an imperfect role model. I know it sounds odd for me to want you to highlight your inherent flaws, but the message to your children is, in fact, actually positive and healthy. When you show yourself to be imperfect and you also show that you are okay with it, you reinforce the message that no one is perfect and that it's actually better not to be. You can send this message in several ways. You can acknowledge, shrug your shoulders, and laugh when you make a mistake ("Oh well, I'm not perfect"). You can share stories from your past in which you made mistakes and failed. Relatedly, you can show your young athletes how those setbacks actually benefited and propelled you to later success. The more they see your own imperfections and hear you accepting them as part of being a human being, the more likely they are to adopt that same attitude and accept their own flaws.

Additionally, many sport parents and their young athletes think mistakes are awful things to be avoided at all costs, despite seeing the most successful athletes in the world make mistakes routinely. Serena Williams double faults, Tom Brady throws interceptions, LeBron James misses shots, and Simone Biles bobbles on the balance beam. These incredible athletes haven't become so successful despite their mistakes and failures, but rather because of them. So, if great athletes make mistakes, it should also not only be expected but also acceptable that your young athletes would make mistakes too.

You need to communicate to your children that mistakes are a natural and necessary part of sports and life. They must accept and learn from their mistakes. Mistakes are guides to what your children need to work on to achieve their goals. Without them, improvement will be a random and undirected process. Mistakes can tell your children that they are taking risks and moving out of their comfort zone. If your young athletes never make mistakes, they are probably not pushing themselves hard enough, they will not improve, and they will never become truly successful.

Finally, there's even a book titled *Perfect Parenting*. What an impossible standard to live up to! But here's some news: You don't need to be a perfect sports parent, just an excellent one (I can hear the collective parental sigh of relief throughout the land). Being an excellent sports parent means being good with your children most of the time; it means supporting them, encouraging them, cheering for them when they succeed, and consoling them when they fail. Being an excellent sports parent also means you can actually make mistakes with your children. You can occasionally lose your temper or show disappointment or act like a stereotypical sports parent. So, cut yourself some slack about being a perfect sports parent. When you are an excellent sports parent, not only will you be happier and have more fun with your children in their athletic lives, but also they will get the message that they can relax and just be the best young athletes they can be, which will lead to more fun and more success for them.

FEAR OF FAILURE

Parents bring their young athletes to me for a variety of reasons, including low confidence and extreme negativity, debilitating precompetitive anxiety, a paralyzing preoccupation with results, or severe self-criticism. In all cases, these challenges are preventing them from performing their best and holding them back from achieving their goals.

In most cases, fear of failure lies at the heart of these symptoms. It causes children to experience doubt, worry, and anxiety, setting themselves up for failure even before they enter the competitive arena. Fear of failure causes them to sabotage their performances with subpar effort and uncommitted and tentative performances, and, ultimately, it prevents them from achieving their athletic goals. After a performance, they are either relieved if they were successful or devastated if they failed.

> The greatest obstacle to success is fear of failure.—*Debasish Mridha, physician and author*[5]

What's So Scary about Failure?

I find it strange to think that children would fear failure when they play sports. The best athletes in the world fail frequently, so why should your young athletes find failure so painful. One classic example is that basketball great Michael Jordan didn't make his junior varsity team. What I've learned in my work with athletes who have a fear of failure is that, they don't actually fear failure. What young athletes come to fear is the meaning they attach to failure. Like perfectionism, your children will develop a fear of failure if they believe that, when they fail, something bad will happen. Research that has investigated fear of failure has found the following as the most common fears among young athletes:

- They will disappoint and upset their parents
- Their parents won't love them
- Their friends will no longer like them
- They will be ostracized by their peer group
- They will experience embarrassment, humiliation, or shame
- They will be worthless people
- Their efforts will have been a waste of time
- They will experience the devastation of not achieving their goals
- They will be failures for life

Young athletes with a fear of failure perceive failure to be a ravenous beast that pursues them relentlessly and must be avoided at all costs. If it catches them, it will eat and kill them. When they do succeed and avoid the beast, they only experience a small and brief amount of relief because they survived one more day without being eaten by failure. As a result, avoiding failure becomes their singular motivation and goal in life.

> Remembering that I'll be dead soon is the most important tool I've ever encountered to help me make the big choices in life. Because almost everything—all external expectations, all pride, all fear of embarrassment or failure—these things just fall away in the face of death, leaving only what is truly important. — *Steve Jobs, tech visionary*[6]

Causes of Fear of Failure

There are three powerful forces in the lives of your young athletes that can cause them to develop a fear of failure. You want to keep your radar on for the messages your children are getting from these three forces to ensure they are getting the right messages.

First, we live in a hypercompetitive youth sports culture in which "You gotta win, baby!" is the constant mantra. Your children are continually being bombarded by messages giving them truly distorted views about success and failure. One message that many young athletes get is that anything less than all-out victory is failure. Because of the internet and social media, the winners are celebrated and the losers demeaned. Our youth sports culture has created a culture of fear and avoidance of failure among young athletes. You want to do everything you can to protect your young athletes from these toxic messages and, as this is very difficult given the connected world in which your children are growing up, make an effort to provide healthier messages that mitigate the destructive messages from our sports culture.

Second, your children's sport programs can become infected by this disease. As I discuss in chapter 1, many youth sports programs have lost perspective on the purpose and value of children playing sports and are now more focused on making money by satisfying the vicarious needs of sport parents who have also lost perspective than giving kids an amazing sports experience. The bar of youth sports participation has been raised so high—"Your kids aren't on a traveling team?!?!"—that success can feel unattainable to many young athletes and, more importantly, suck the fun out of what should be a really fun experience. The end result is that many children choose to quit youth sports rather than suffer the indignities heaped upon them by our youth sports culture.

Finally, you don't want to fall under our youth sports culture's spell of failure. It's become an almost daily occurrence to read about some parent going berserk at their children's games, either getting into a fight with another parent, abusing a ref, or yelling at their kid. They've compounded the harm our youth sports culture can inflict on young athletes by becoming overly invested in their athletic lives (think Little League parents) to such an extent that, as I note earlier in this chapter, their self-esteem becomes dependent on their children's athletic success. Many parents also unwittingly connect their own love and approval of their children to whether their children succeed or fail. The message young athletes often receive from their parents (however unintentionally) is, "I won't love you if you lose," either indirectly through their parents' emotional reactions (e.g., anger, frustration, disappointment, embarrassment) or directly through what they say to them ("Why did you play so poorly?" said with an angry tone). Athletes come to see failure as a threat to their very value as people, their status within their family, and their place in society as a whole.

In essence, young athletes with a fear of failure see failure, as mentioned earlier, as a mountain lion that, if it catches them, it will eat them. Given this perception of failure, it's not surprising that they would do everything they can to stay as far away from that mountain lion as possible. But here's a brief hint before we sink our teeth into this topic (pun intended): Failure is a kitty cat, not a mountain lion. Yes, a kitty cat can hurt your children; it can scratch and bite them. But, and here's the big point for young athletes with a fear of failure, it won't kill them.

If these messages from parents persist, young athletes internalize them and make them their own. At some point, they no longer need their parents to send those messages. Instead, the children view themselves through the lens of their parents' criticism and send those same messages to themselves in the form of unrelenting judgment and self-criticism. The end result is a genuinely unpleasant sports experience and potentially long-term harm to children's athletic and personal development.

The Gift of Failure

Contrary to what our youth sports culture may tell you, failure is actually a gift you can give your young athletes as they pursue their sports goals because failure is an inevitable—and essential—part of sports and life. How so, you may ask? Failure can bolster your children's motivation to overcome the obstacles that caused the failure. It shows them what they did wrong so they can correct the problem in the future. Failure connects your children's efforts with their outcomes, which helps them gain ownership of their sports participation. Failure teaches such important life skills as commitment, patience, perseverance, determination, and problem solving. It helps children respond positively to the frustration and disappointment they will often experience as they pursue their goals. Failure teaches children humility and appreciation for the opportunities they're given.

Of course, too much failure will discourage young athletes because success is one of the rewarding aspects of sports participation, and, quite simply, it's no fun to lose all of the time. Success is also needed for its ability to bolster motivation, build confidence, reinforce effort, and increase enjoyment. As your children pursue their athletic goals, they must experience a healthy balance of success and failure to gain the most from their efforts.

You can help your young athletes develop a healthy perspective on failure that takes away their fear. It also frees them to strive for success without fear, doubt, or worry, and with commitment, confidence, and courage. Your goal is to raise children who know in their hearts that some failure is okay and in no way an immovable obstacle in the path to their goals or a negative reflection on themselves as people.

> I've failed over and over again in my life, and that is why I succeed. —*Michael Jordan, basketball legend*[7]

Failure will ultimately enable your young athletes to achieve success, however they define it, and, along the way, also find happiness in their sports experiences.

How Young Athletes Avoid Failure

Young athletes who struggle with a fear of failure are not focused on achieving success, but rather their primary motivation in their sports participation is to avoid failure because they see it as a truly threatening outcome. These children learn they can avoid failure in three ways. First, they can simply not play their sport in which they are experiencing the fear of failure. If children don't play, they can't fail. And, although there is no decisive research on this, it isn't a stretch to attribute the 70 percent dropout rate in youth sports by the time kids are 13 years old in part to fear of failure and related indignities that young athletes experience in their sports involvement. Injury; illness; forgotten, lost, or damaged equipment; apparent lack of interest or motivation; or just plain quitting are common ways in which young athletes can avoid failure and maintain their personal and social esteem.

Second, young athletes can also protect themselves from the perceived consequences of failure by actually causing themselves to fail (usually unconsciously) in their sport but protecting themselves from the failure by having an excuse—"I would have done well, but my knee hurt so bad" or "I would have won, but I'm so stressed out with school." This defensive reaction is called self-defeating behavior or self-sabotage. Because their failures were not their fault (they can blame factors outside of themselves), children feel absolved of responsibility, and the youth sports culture, their peers, and their parents must continue, as they see it, to accept and love them.

Third, many young athletes don't have the luxury of quitting—their parents won't let them—or coming up with excuses. So, another way they can avoid failure is to get as far away from failure as possible by becoming successful. But children who are driven to avoid failure are stuck in limbo between failure and real success, what I call the "safety zone," in which the threat of failure is removed by being pretty good athletes. In other words, they are far from failure. For example, they finish in the top 10 in their sport or have a winning record, so no one can call them real failures. At the same time, they are unwilling to intensify their efforts and take the risks necessary to achieve true success.

There is clearly a cost to be paid by young athletes who use any of these strategies (again, almost always unconsciously) to avoid failure. Most obviously, they fail to both enjoy their sports experiences and, regardless of the excuses they have, achieve the athletic goals they had set for themselves. Plus, they not only miss out on the wonderful emotions they will experience in their sports efforts—excitement, joy, pride, inspiration—but also they are wracked with many negative emotions, including disappointment, sadness, and regret, at having not given their best effort and at least tried to achieve their goals.

Fear of Total Failure

As I explored fear of failure in the young athletes I work with, I was struck by an odd paradox. These children have a fear of failure. Yet, they end up doing things that actually cause themselves to fail (e.g., have a pessimistic attitude, don't prepare well, or don't give their best effort), even when success is within their reach. Moreover, when they engage in self-sabotage, they create a lose–lose situation for themselves: They not only fail to achieve their sports goals, but also they feel great disappointment and regret because they didn't even give themselves a chance. I was stumped by this conflict: Why would young athletes who fear failure so much actually do things that guarantee failure and create this lose–lose experience for themselves?

The failure I just described, which is a form of self-sabotage, safeguards athletes from having to admit they really failed by providing an excuse for their failure. That excuse allows them to avoid taking responsibility for the failure, protecting them from feeling like a failure and feeling worthless. One big problem with this strategy is that they still fail. And there is no "excuse" line on the result sheet.

As you consider whether your young athletes have a fear of failure and how it might affect them, it's important to understand something I came to realize, namely, that they don't really have a fear of failure, but rather a fear of *total* failure. Let me clarify the difference for you. Total failure means that young athletes give their best effort and don't achieve their goals. Another way to help you see the difference is that with total failure, they can't make any excuses that might protect them from failure because they did the best they could. I have asked many young athletes what they think of total failure, and their response is almost unanimous: It is the worst! If children give their fullest effort and still fail, they have to admit they just aren't good enough and there's nothing more they can do. No young athlete wants to admit, much less accept, they don't have the "goods." Strangely, children with a fear of total failure believe it's better to fail with an excuse than to fail having done their best that day because it allows them to avoid the consequences of total failure (e.g., disappointing others, wasting time, being embarrassed) and always leaves open the possibility of success in the future.

Yet, contrary to what most young athletes believe, I would argue that total failure is a good (although not ideal) goal for them to aspire to. Even though they may not fully reach their sports goals, they will have done everything they could to get as far as they can, and, ultimately, that's all they can do. Plus, your children will experience the pride in having given their best effort. Unlike the lose–lose scenario I described earlier, striving for total failure creates a win–win, in which young athletes first win by feeling good about having given their all and then they get at least a partial win by making progress toward their sports goals (they may or may not fully achieve the goals).

You want to convince your young athletes that total failure, far from being the worst thing that can happen, is actually a good thing (although, obviously not the best thing). Let's compare total failure to total success, which happens when your children give it everything they have and achieve their goal. Clearly, total success is a very good thing. But what makes total failure not nearly so awful for young athletes is that it shares one important thing with total success. In both cases, they give it their all, and at the end of the day, that's all your children can do when they compete. Sometimes, they win, other times, they lose. Of course, they will be disappointed if they give their best effort. At the same time, there will also be indelible satisfaction and pride at having done their best and performed as well as they possibly could have. And only by experiencing that "total something" do your young athletes have any chance of finding success in the long run.

The Fear That Underlies Fear of Failure

As I have worked more and more with young athletes with a fear of failure, I haved delved deeply into what underlies this self-defeating behavior. Not long ago, I had another surprising insight about fear of failure that gave me a new and even deeper understanding of what is really at the heart of fear of failure. As I peeled back the layers of the onion, I've realized that the real fear is not failure itself or the meaning young athletes attach to it, or even the total failure I just described. Instead, the real fear of failure that can be so debilitating for children when they compete is the fear of experiencing the painful emotions that can come with total failure, including humiliation, shame, sadness, guilt, and frustration. If your young athletes have a fear of failure, so much of their energy is devoted to avoiding those truly unpleasant emotions they are so certain will surely come if they experience total failure.

Sadly, if your young athletes have a fear of failure, they suffer unnecessarily for several reasons. First, the chances are that your children's belief that they will experience these painful emotions are pretty low. In all likelihood, you will continue to love and support them. Their friends will still like them. They will still be worthwhile people who are valued by others. And they won't be labeled losers for life because their efforts as athletes will teach them valuable life lessons they can use as they pursue their goals in other avenues of their lives.

Second, your young athletes' fear of failure actually prevents them from ever finding the success you know they want so much. They perform below their capabilities. They are both confused and mad at themselves for not doing their best. And they continue to think, feel, and perform in ways that make their sports experiences the opposite of fun and thwart their efforts to achieve their athletic goals.

Third, if you can help your children to unburden themselves of their fear of failure and really give their best efforts, the odds are very good that they will find some success. I can't say how much success because a lot of things beyond the mind determine how successful young athletes become, but, as I often say, good things would happen.

Moreover, if your young athletes would be willing to put themselves out there and risk total failure, instead of being overwhelmed by the painful emotions I describe here, they would actually feel wonderful emotions, for instance, excitement, elation, pride, and inspiration, for having the courage to confront and overcome their fears.

In sum, one of the greatest gifts you can give your young athletes is the message that failure, although not ideal, is essential for success, so they would be able to say, "To achieve total success, I must be willing to accept total failure." With this liberating attitude, your children would no longer fear failure and be free to pursue their athletic goals with unrestrained vigor.

> We don't fear failure. We fear shame. — *Whitney English, corporate coach*[8]

You Have the Power

A basic tenet of mine about child development is that parents have an immense influence on their children. Yes, you give your kids your genes, which certainly impacts who they become. At the same time, how you raise them matters too, especially in how they come to view their sports experiences. What this means is that young athletes aren't born with a fear of failure. Instead, one way they develop their attitudes toward and beliefs about failure is from the world around them, primarily from the youth sports culture and the athletic programs of which they are members, and from you.

Some of those harmful messages about failure come from our youth sports culture, which has lost perspective on why children play sports. These messages are disseminated by a sports media that worships at the altar of success and overly competitive youth sports programs and their coaches who give winning greater importance than fun and youth development. As I note in chapter 1, you have the power to determine what sort of youth sports culture your young athletes are surrounded by and the athletic programs you place them in.

But, as sad as it is to say, fear of failure in young athletes usually comes from their parents, who communicate that failure is unacceptable in several ways. First, as role models, you might do this by reacting to your own failures with self-criticism, anger, and despondency. In observing how you respond to failure in this way, they get the subtle, yet unmistakable, message that, "My mom [dad] hates failure, so I better not fail."

Second, you can do this by sending direct messages to your children that failure is simply unacceptable. When all you talk about before and after games is winning or losing, and when you say things like, "You better win today" or "I can't believe you lost," the message is crystal clear to your children what is important to you. And what is important to you usually becomes what is important to them.

And, third, you might do this by your unconscious emotional reactions as you share your children's athletic lives. For example, you might be stressed out before a game or lose your temper after a losing effort. Children, particularly at a young age, are more intuitive than cerebral, meaning they are more attuned to your emotions than your words. If you're upset, no matter what you say, your kids will hone in on those emotions. The message your young athletes get, whether through role modeling, direct messages, or your emotions, is, "I can't lose or I'll really upset my parents." The more harmful subtext of this statement, which is so difficult for parents to believe, is, "If I lose, my parents won't love me." And there is nothing more fear-inducing for children than thinking they could lose their parents' love.

This is quite depressing, to be sure. But here's the good news: If you can send unhealthy messages to your young athletes, you also have the power to send healthy ones. And that is where you can first begin to give your young athletes a sports experience free from fear of failure or relieve them of the burden of fear of failure.

What You Can Do

After giving a workshop on fear of failure to a group of parents a while back, I received an e-mail from an attendee asking an important question: "I now understand why my child keeps getting in his own way. He has a fear of failure! So, what can I do about it?" Let me share some ways in which you can help your young athletes to let go of their fear of failure.

Let me preface my thoughts by saying that there are entire books devoted to fear of failure and how to overcome it. Also, in severe cases, psychotherapy may be warranted. My point is that, as with most things in life, there are no magic pills for or quick fixes to fear of failure. At the same time, there are some simple steps you can take to prevent your children from developing this fear or relieve them of the burden, so they can pursue success without reservation or hesitation and with courage and commitment.

The best way to put your young athletes on a healthy path toward enjoyment and success in their sports lives is to make sure you have a healthy perspective about why they are involved in sports (see chapter 1 for more on this). When you focus on the wonderful benefits of your kids playing sports and downplay the importance of winning and losing, you are setting your children up for both a positive and fun sports experience, and the opportunity to find success in their efforts. If you can send your children healthy messages about failure from the start of their sports participation or make changes in a positive direction if they're already involved, they will get these messages and begin to shift how they think and feel about failure.

The first step in helping your young athletes develop a healthy relationship with failure is for you to have a healthy relationship with failure. I assume you've experienced failure in your own life, whether at work or perhaps in your own athletic life. When you do experience setbacks, how do you respond? To be a positive role model for your children, you want to ensure that you react to failure in a calm, accepting, and constructive way. For example, if you're a tennis player and lose a match against someone whom you thought you would beat, are you able to smile and shrug it off? Having your kids "do as I do" is a powerful way you can shape their attitudes toward and reactions to failure.

Your actions clearly matter, but so do your words. When you combine "do as I say" with "do as I do," you send your young athletes a powerful one–two punch for a healthy attitude toward failure. So, talk to your kids about how our youth sports culture unhealthily defines failure, explain why it's not good, and offer them a healthy definition of failure and why it's better. You can also describe how those definitions play out in real life, comparing the thinking, emotions, and reactions that follow a healthy and unhealthy view of failure. The more your children can understand both sides of failure, the better able they will be to make good choices on how they think, feel, and respond to the failure they will inevitably experience in their athletic lives.

Another formidable way to impress a healthy attitude toward failure on your young athletes is to show them examples of successful athletes (and people in other fields) who have overcome failure on the way to success. Tom Brady wasn't drafted until the seventh round. And Michelle Wie struggled mightily early in her LPGA career before rising to the top. If you're a sports fan, you can find examples every day of athletes who overcame great failure before finding great success.

In an ideal world in which we are all perfect beings, all of us parents would take my advice to heart and be total Zen masters about our children's sports participation; we would always be positive, calm, and composed whenever we watch them play. But we don't live in an ideal world and most of us are, in fact, truly imperfect beings. Most of us carry baggage related to success and failure from our childhoods, most of us are vulnerable to the messages we get from the youth sports culture, and, regardless, all of us want our kids to find success in their athletic lives, so it's upsetting to see them fail. Given that, like most parents, you might very well be an imperfect being, here are some practical things you can do when watching your young athletes compete to ensure that the pain you feel at their failures, if any, doesn't come through and interfere with their developing a positive relationship with failure.

Perhaps the toughest thing you need to do is look in the mirror. I don't mean literally, but to reflect on yourself openly and honestly about your strengths and areas in need of improvement related to failure. You may find that you send really good messages about failure to your young athletes. Or, you may have to admit that there isn't always joy in Whoville, that is, you have discomfort with your children's failures and may communicate that discomfort to them in some way. Ask yourself what messages about failure you might be conveying to your children, directly or indirectly, and in what situations you are sending them. If you have a spouse or partner, it can also be helpful to get some feedback from them, as they may see reactions in you that you aren't even aware of.

If you feel that you're doing good things related to these three situations, keep doing what you're doing because you're sending great messages about failure to your kids. But, if you're not, you have short-term and long-term options. First, in the short term, stay home. I realize that this is tough advice, but it's advice I have given often and been thanked for doing so later. You will do far less harm not being there and have time to decompress and regain perspective before your kids arrive home after the game. Even if you think you have your emotions under control, you probably don't. You may have a smile on your face and you may be saying, "Good job," but your face will be gnarled with pain and your body wracked with tension. There is no hiding from those emotions. If you can't control your emotions when you're watching your children compete, they will pick up on your emotions before, during, and after the game, and, as I just discussed, these unhealthy messages will come through loud and clear to them.

Second, if you're ready to confront your failure demons, you can work to change the way you think, feel, and react to failure and, in doing so, shift your messages to your young athletes from unhealthy to healthy. As already noted, there are no quick fixes or easy solutions. In its simplest form, this transformation involves recognizing that you're hurting your children, making a commitment to the change, and replacing old and unhealthy attitudes with new and healthy ones, and old emotions and behaviors with new ones. There are, as they say, many roads to Rome; reading a book like *Raising Young Athletes*, attending sport parenting workshops, seeking out a parent coach, or going to see a psychotherapist or psychologist are potentially effective ways to get there.

At a basic level, the first step, once you've identified your unhealthy reactions, is to specify the sports situations in which they arise. This allows you to know when your "hot buttons" are going to be pushed, making it easier to prepare for it when it happens. Next, figure out the alternative healthier ways in which you want to react. Consider how you want to change your thinking (from "She better win today" to "I hope she has fun today"), your emotions (from anxiety and dread to excitement and pride), what you say to your kids (from "You have to win today" to "Do your best"), and your behavior (pacing the sidelines and yelling at the ref to sitting calmly and cheering for everyone). Then, make a plan for how you want to be at the game and imagine yourself executing that plan. Perhaps enlist your spouse or partner to encourage you and remind you of your plan. Finally, as the game nears, make a conscious commitment to use the new approaches through to their conclusion and put your plan into action. I can assure you that making this shift will be exceedingly difficult at first, but, in time, the more you take the "good road," the easier it will be and the better it will feel. And, as much as your old habits may pull you back down the "bad road," what more incentive do you need than the health and well-being of your children and your relationship with them?

And here's another piece of advice that is going to be tough to follow, but it is another wonderful gift you can give to your young athletes: Never talk about results. Here's a simple reality: Your children can't develop a fear of failure if failure is never discussed. Instead of talking about results, always focus on the process (e.g., what they did, their effort) and the fun of their sports participation. The powerful message your children will get is that you don't care about results, success or failure, so they shouldn't either.

Of course, your refusal to discuss results isn't going to stop your young athletes from wanting to talk about them. They are surrounded by a youth sports culture telling them that results matter (and, realistically, they do to some extent). It is nearly impossible to completely protect your young athletes from being "carpet bombed" with unhealthy messages from coaches, parents, and their peers who are obsessed with results. If you've ever been to any youth sports competition, you know most of the conversations among parents are about results, rankings, and won–loss records. And, sadly, I see the same thing happening to the young competitors. This is not a surprise given my belief that children tend to adopt the attitudes of their parents, healthy or not.

Although you can't be your children's impenetrable shield against these influences, you can at least play defense and block or blunt a lot of the fear-of-failure barbs thrown at them. You need to counteract those unhealthy messages with positive messages of your own. So, when they do bring up results, whether after a game or at dinner, redirect the conversation to, you guessed it, anything related to the process or fun of their sport. Plus, as noted earlier, when you surround your young athletes with a like-minded sports program and like-minded parents and peers, you can all work together to protect them from the harmful messages about failure of our off-the-rails youth sports culture.

EMOTIONS

Emotions play a vital role in youth sports. Athletic participation means experiencing frequent and powerful emotions, often within the span of a few minutes. From the thrill of victory to the agony of defeat, young athletes revel in the excitement, elation, joy, pride, and inspiration of competing in sports. Less pleasantly, they also experience fear, disappointment, frustration, anger, and despair. As a parent, you want your children to experience all of the positive emotions and none of the negative ones. We love to see them happy and excited. And it pains us to see them in emotional pain.

But, in viewing their athletic lives through a wider lens, you actually want your young athletes to feel all of the emotions, both good and less so, because that is what makes youth sports so impactful and, ultimately, important to their overall and long-term development as both athletes and people.

Emotions are, in fact, two sides of the same coin. Your children can't cherry pick the emotions they want to experience in their athletic lives. They must either experience them all or none at all. So, it's not a matter of what emotions you want them to feel. Rather, what you do have a choice in is doing everything you can to ensure your children's sports experiences result in emotions that are mostly positive and, when they aren't, the less-pleasant emotions build determination and resilience rather than lead to hurt and abandonment of their sports participation. That influence includes what emotions you trigger in them and how you respond to the myriad of emotions they are certain to experience as they enter and immerse themselves in their sports.

Emotions in sports are important because those that are most powerful and prevalent will determine your children's perceptions about, attitudes toward, and reactions to their athletic lives. In other words, their emotions act as the lens through which they look at their sports participation. Positive emotions about playing sports foster positive perceptions about your young athletes' athletic lives and encourage further commitment to and effort in achieving their sports goals. Children who have positive experiences come to associate sports with such emotions as excitement, satisfaction, and happiness.

Although negative emotions like frustration and disappointment are a natural and healthy part of young athletes pursuing their own personal greatness, excessively negative and intense emotions, for instance, fear and despair, can cause them to connect their efforts with feeling bad, which will ultimately discourage their interest and efforts in pursuing their athletic goals. Unhealthy negative emotions are, in fact, a significant obstacle to having a positive sports experience because the feelings are so forceful, immediate, and unpleasant. Strong and persistent negative emotions affect children at many levels, including sapping their motivation, undermining their confidence, blurring their focus, and causing competitive anxiety.

Your young athletes' emotional reactions to their efforts on the playing field develop as they accumulate experiences in their sports participation. These emotional responses take shape as attitudes that your children hold about their athletic lives. Unhealthy emotions that are recurrent and intense lead to harmful attitudes commonly known as the "baggage" that children develop and carry with them throughout their sports experiences and, even more harmfully, into other aspects of their lives and adulthood.

One of the most difficult aspects of unhealthy emotions in sports is that they become ingrained, so they cause children to automatically respond to an athletic experience with a particular preprogrammed emotional reaction, even when that emotional response does more harm than good. For example, a young tennis player is constantly chastised by her father for losing matches. In time, she comes to fear walking onto the tennis court because she knows if she plays poorly, her father will be angry with her. This fear actually causes the thing she fears the most to happen, namely, losing and incurring her father's wrath. Moreover, this reaction seeps into other settings, notably at school, where she develops tremendous performance anxiety before tests.

The kinds of emotional reactions your young athletes have in response to their sports participation depend on everything I have discussed up to this point. What you do in the development of your children's sense of self and feelings of ownership will determine the emotions they will experience in their athletic lives. Then, in a circular manner, these emotions determine

> A ballplayer who loses his head and can't keep his cool is worse than no player at all. —*Lou Gehrig, baseball legend*[9]

your sense of self and ownership, causing either a virtuous or vicious cycle that will color their future sports and, possibly, broader life experiences.

Warning Signs of Emotions

One thing about emotions is they are felt by your young athletes with such immediacy and force. Another thing is that these emotions aren't easy to miss, so it's not difficult to see when your kids are struggling emotionally in their athletic lives. There are several warning signs you should look for in your children to evaluate their emotional experiences in sports.

One of the clearest signs of emotional difficulties related to sports is anxiety before competitions. It's natural for all athletes to feel some nerves before they compete because they are putting their efforts to the test and there are no guarantees those efforts will be rewarded. But, when those feelings are aversive and interfere with young athletes' ability to perform their best and enjoy the experiences, you should take note and take action. Muscle tension, short and choppy breathing, stiff movement, social withdrawal, that "deer in the headlights" look in their eyes before a competition, as well as tentative performances during competitions, are a few of the indications of competitive anxiety.

Another warning sign is emotions that are extreme, out of control, or out of proportion to the athletic situation your children are in, for example, young athletes who are terrified of going onto the field to compete, have uncontrollable anger or tears after a loss, or exhibit sadness and dejection days after a poor performance. These emotional reactions are powerful indicators of some unhealthy attitudes toward sports, and these attitudes can become significant obstacles to young athletes pursuing their sports goals.

Two of the most common reactions to persistent negative emotional experiences on the part of young athletes are reluctance to walk onto the field of play to compete (e.g., "I don't feel like playing today"), coming up with excuses not to compete (e.g., illness or injury), or an outright avoidance of competing (e.g., "I don't like [insert sport here] anymore"). These responses are strong signs that your children's athletic experiences are truly negative to the extent that they no longer want to participate.

Lastly, a truly unfortunate emotional reaction to negative sports experiences involves what I call "unhappy successes." These are young athletes who respond to the threatening emotions (usually grounded in fear of failure) by pursuing success with desperate determination and finding temporary relief in those successes. But they pay a price in unhappiness. Rather than experiencing elation and pride in their efforts, the best emotion these children can muster is relief that is short-lived for having avoided the threat that was causing the unhealthy emotions.

What You Can Do

So, the signs of emotional difficulties in children related to their sports participation are usually quite clear. A greater challenge for you, however, is seeing the
considerable impact your emotions have on your young athletes. You have to
recognize that children are visceral beings who, because they haven't fully developed cognitively or intellectually, are highly attuned to their parents' emotional
messages. So, it's important that the emotional messages you send your young
athletes support healthy emotional experiences in their sports participation.

You want to start with your emotional reactions to your children's athletic
successes and failures. One of the biggest emotional warning signs I see from
parents at competitions is emotions that are stronger than those of their children. Here's a simple test: Do you get more excited than your children after
they win, and do you get more despondent than them when they lose? Do you
feel their victories and losses are yours as much as theirs? If you answered yes
to these questions, you are probably not sending healthy emotional messages to
your kids. What's the message? That how they perform makes you either really
happy or really unhappy? And that can be a crushing weight on the shoulders
of your young athletes and produce in them the emotional difficulties described
earlier in this chapter.

Another warning sign is emotional overprotection on your part, that is, your
need to shield your young athletes from feeling bad when they fail. As parents,
we hate to see our children feel disap-
pointed, sad, frustrated, or angry. So,
what do we do? We placate, assuage,
distract, comfort, and, in general, do
everything we can to make them happy
again. Yet, in our attempts at protecting them from the harsh realities of
sports (and life), we do a disservice to

> Emotional hurt, you gotta let that
> go. Walk away and let it be. So
> many highs and lows, but if you
> keep being down, you'll never
> get up. —*Micky Ward, former
> professional boxer*[10]

their long-term development. As painful as it can be for you as a parent, you
want your kids to feel bad when they do poorly because those feelings are essential for their developing emotional mastery.

What Is Emotional Mastery?

Let me begin by explaining what emotional mastery is *not* for your young athletes. It is not suppressing their emotions, not feeling their emotions, or avoiding their emotions. To the contrary, your children can't develop emotional

mastery without their fully experiencing the full range of emotions, from excitement and joy to frustration and dejection. From these emotional experiences, they become familiar and comfortable with their emotions, from which they can then develop the skills to master their emotions.

Emotional mastery involves several steps. First, as I just noted, you should help your young athletes be fully open to their emotional lives, experience the full range of emotions, and feel all emotions deeply. Second, when they feel emotions, they should not only be capable of knowing that the emotions are either good or bad, pleasant or unpleasant, but also identifying what those specific emotions are. For example, after a competitive loss, your children will certainly feel bad, but emotional mastery involves their being able to label the emotion. Is what they feel disappointment, hurt, embarrassment, or frustration? By labeling their emotions, your kids take the first step toward emotional mastery because they can now take what are often vague and amorphous experiences and make them more tangible and, as a result, more within their control.

Once the specific emotions have been identified, the next step in emotional mastery is for your young athletes to understand where they came from in their sports experience. For instance, if what they feel is embarrassment after a loss, why do they feel that emotion? Do they feel they underperformed? Do they feel they were letting down their parents? Are they concerned others will judge them to be failures? This understanding of the emotions your children feel allows them to make the emotions even more tangible and put them in a greater context, enabling them to decide how to respond to the emotions.

There are two typical problems with how children deal with the emotions they experience in sports (and life in general). First, they keep their emotions bottled up inside of them. Particularly in sports and among boys, emotional expression, especially of the negative variety, goes against the ethos of both sport and masculinity and is often viewed as a sign of weakness. Unfortunately, this strategy rarely works for emotions of any degree of intensity because they have to be released somehow, so these suppressed emotions seep out indirectly by, for example, internally directed depression, general irritability, or misdirected anger, none of which honor, healthily express, or resolve the emotions.

Second, the emotions are expressed strongly and indiscriminately. For instance, a young athlete who is angered about a loss to a rival lashes out at his coach, which, of course, only angers the coach and doesn't get at the real emotions underlying the anger, namely, hurt and disappointment at the loss. Moreover, these two unproductive ways of dealing with emotions don't help in providing a solution to the problem that caused the emotions. And, they may damage the athlete's relationship with his coach.

Are You an Emotional Master?

A consistent theme of this chapter is that you are largely responsible for how your children develop both as athletes and people. That influence is no less important to their emotional life, and you should do everything you can to support their development into emotional masters. As with many aspects of *Raising Young Athletes*, the first way to positively impact your children in their athletic lives is to look inward and see what influence you have on them, in this case, on their emotional development. You can examine the emotional impact you have on your children—both positive and negative—and identify what you may need to change to foster their emotional growth. For example, if you get upset when your kids lose, you need to step back, acknowledge your reactions aren't helping them, and examine why you have such strong emotional reactions.

Be a Positive Role Model

Your greatest influence on your children's emotional development is as a role model; what you feel, say, and do acts as their template for how they should respond to themselves and their world. Raising emotional masters is greatly facilitated when you possess the qualities you want to see in your young athletes. Your children will learn their most basic emotional habits from you through observation. If you lack emotional mastery and control, it is likely that, unless they have other strong role models to influence them, they too will develop the same emotional challenges as you have.

If you as a parent are an emotional master, you have a good start on instilling positive emotional habits in your children. You are more likely to be a positive influence on your children's sports experience because you will maintain a healthy perspective on your children's athletic lives and react to their inevitable ups and downs in balanced and reasonable ways. You will have greater awareness of your own emotional needs and the capacity to control them for the best interests of the children. You will also not be working at odds with the children's needs and goals. As a result, your goals and efforts will align with theirs, and they will feel encouraged and supported emotionally as they attempt to navigate the emotionally challenging seas of competitive sports.

If you are an emotional master, you will, from the start, teach your young

> Parents are the ultimate role models for children. Every word, movement, and action has an effect. No other person or outside force has a greater influence on a child than the parent. —Bob Keeshan, actor[11]

athletes healthy emotional habits that will foster their growth both as athletes and young people. You will not only "talk the talk" on emotional mastery but also "walk the walk"—you will act as a positive role model, displaying the emotional habits your children should learn to become emotional masters themselves.

Know Your Baggage

One of the greatest gifts you can give your children is actually something you don't give them, namely, your emotional baggage. Let me explain. As a human being, you bring a lot of great things from your upbringing, including healthy values, attitudes, and passions. At the same time, also as a human being, you likely bring some not-so-good things from childhood—your emotional baggage—insecurities, fears, and worries. Examples of common emotional baggage include perfectionism, fear of failure, self-criticism, low self-esteem, the need to please, the need to control, and concern for what others think of you, just to name a few. Sadly, also as a human being, you can inadvertently pass your emotional baggage on to your children if you don't do something to stop its transmission. An essential goal for you is to not give your children your baggage; they'll get their own because that's the way people are.

The key lesson here is to know your baggage. If you know your emotional baggage, you are less likely to pass it on to your children. There are many ways you can identify and mitigate your baggage, including psychotherapy, self-help books and videos, seminars, and meditation. I operate based on the assumption that all parents have emotional baggage, so I recommend that all parents explore, identify, and resolve that baggage preemptively before it starts showing up in your children's lives, both on and off the field of play.

Developing Emotional Mastery in Your Children

Your young athletes becoming emotional masters involves their developing the ability to understand their emotional lives and make healthy choices about what emotions they feel, how they react to those emotions, and how they express them. Your children can easily understand, enjoy, and express positive emotions—happiness, pride, inspiration. The difficulty for them is to experience negative emotions—frus-

> Our emotions need to be as educated as our intellect. It is important to know how to feel, how to respond, and how to let life in so that it can touch you.
> —*Anonymous*[12]

tration, anger, sadness—and react to and express them in ways that encourage rather than detract from their athletic efforts, enjoyment of their sport, overall development as people, and general happiness.

Let Them Feel All of Their Emotions

There are a number of strategies you can use to guide your young athletes toward emotional mastery in their athletic lives and their lives beyond sports. The first step is to allow your children to feel all of their emotions, whether good, bad, or ugly. As I mentioned earlier, the mama or papa bear in all of us wants to make our kids always feel good, and we feel their pain deeply when they feel bad. But your children can't develop emotional mastery if you don't give them the space to feel all of their emotions deeply. So, for example, instead of rushing to your sad young athletes after a tough loss, let them just be with what they're feeling. Yes, they will feel bad, and, yes, you will feel bad seeing your children feeling bad. Yet, in resisting your natural parental urges to protect kids from pain and focusing on the emotional "long game," you give them the freedom to experience the full range of the emotional spectrum. In doing so, you give them the opportunity to explore, identify, and understand their emotions. From this deep understanding, your children can then learn to gain mastery of the emotions they will regularly experience in their athletic and personal lives.

Acknowledge Their Emotions

One of the most common reactions I see from parents when their children are sad, afraid, frustrated, or angry is to dismiss the emotions: "There's nothing to be scared of," "It's no big deal," or "Don't worry about it." Somehow, many parents think that downplaying these emotions their children feel will enable them to suddenly let go of them and feel happy again. But these sorts of reactions actually add insult to injury. Your kids not only feel bad but also feel as if there is something wrong with them because you're telling them they shouldn't be feeling what they're feeling.

Be Real about Their Emotions

You can go another step further in enabling your young athletes to fully experience their emotions by being real about their emotions, in other words, acknowledging rather than minimizing or dismissing them: "You sure are upset about losing your match," "I can see how disappointing it must feel to get beaten today," or "Going that fast can be really scary." When you recognize all of your children's emotions, you're sending the message that you "get" what they're feeling, that it's okay to feel the emotions, and that you're there to support them even during the tough times in their athletic lives.

Be an Emotional Coach

The final piece of emotional mastery involves your offering your young athletes emotional coaching as they experience the emotional challenges of youth sports competition. Emotional mastery is a skill, like any sports skill. You wouldn't want your children to learn new technical or tactical skills in their sport randomly or by trial and error. Instead, you ensure they are properly coached early in their sports participation and taught the essential sports skills in a structured and progressive way so they ingrain and use the skills effectively in competition rather than developing bad habits that are hard to break. Emotional mastery is no different.

Emotional coaching involves several steps in which you give your young athletes experiences, insights, information, and tools to better handle the emotional challenges they face every day in their athletic lives. The first step involves offering them empathy so they see that you understand what they're feeling. Empathy instills trust and comfort in your children, which encourage them to feel their emotions deeply and let you into their emotional world. Once inside, they will be willing to open up about the emotions they are experiencing which creates the opportunity for your emotional coaching.

One powerful tool of emotional coaching is providing your young athletes with a healthy perspective on their emotions. You should recognize that your children will view their emotions in a very narrow way because, due to their youth, they lack the experience with which to put those emotions in context. As a consequence, the emotions are very present, very powerful, and very all encompassing. You can soften the emotions' impact on your young athletes by providing perspective on the situation that caused them—often a painful defeat—and placing them in a longer-term context that makes what feels so big, overwhelming, and insurmountable into something smaller, more manageable, and more readily capable of being overcome.

This shift in perspective toward their emotions is an important step in emotional mastery because it softens the pain of the feelings and offers young athletes a strategy—looking at the emotions in a broader and longer-term way— that can be used in the future when they are faced with other difficult emotions.

With a more positive and hopeful perspective established with your children, they will feel more calm and optimistic about the situation. They will be better positioned to explore their emotions in a more rational way. In the ensuing discussion, you can ask your young athletes the following questions:

- What does the emotion feel like to you (where in your body do you feel it and what does it feel like physically)?
- What emotion are you feeling (hint: it's often not the one you think it is)?
- What caused the emotion?
- Does the emotion seem appropriate for the athletic situation that caused it?
- What is the range of different ways you might react to the emotion?
- What do you think the healthiest reaction to the emotion is that would make you feel better and prepare you to respond to a similar sports situation in a more effective way?
- What strategies can you use the next time you are faced with difficult emotions in your sport?

These explorations into your young athletes' emotional lives teach them how to ask similar questions without you whenever they are confronted with unpleasant emotions stemming from their sports experiences. As they gain experience in asking and answering these questions on their own, they develop the ability to recognize the emotions for what they are and understand their causes. The culmination of this process of gaining emotional mastery is your young athletes' ability to make healthy choices about how emotion-inducing athletic experiences—whether the excitement of an unexpected victory or the pain of an unexpected defeat—will impact them and how they will react to them. And, as with the other pillars I discuss in this chapter, this newly developed emotional mastery is a gift that keeps on giving in all aspects of your children's lives and their future lives.

EXPECTATIONS

Imagine that your young athletes are about to begin a competition and you walk up to them and force them to put on a 50-pound weight vest. How will they feel? Heavy, sluggish, slow. How will they perform? Poorly, to be sure. Well, when you create expectations for your children in their athletic lives, you are placing a metaphorical weight vest on them that will also weigh them down in how they think, feel, and perform. And that is a burden you definitely don't want to place on them.

The great thing is, if you once placed that figurative weight on your children's shoulders, you have the power to remove it. Your goal is to ensure that your children never put that weight vest on, or, if for some reason they do, that they can take it off quickly and easily. This freedom from expectations will allow your young athletes to throw themselves into the mix on their par-

> Too many disappointments are usually a sign of too many expectations. —*Anonymous*[13]

ticular field of play with no doubt, worry, or hesitation and with commitment, confidence, and courage. How will they feel then? Light and unencumbered. How will they perform? Free and strong.

What Are Expectations?

At first glance, setting expectations for your young athletes seems like a good idea because they establish a standard toward which they can strive. At the same time, if you set the wrong types of expectations for your children, you are creating a situation in which you are actually dampening, rather than inspiring, their efforts.

As I begin this discussion, I want to make sure we have a shared understanding of what expectations are: "A strong belief that something will happen in the future . . . a belief that someone will or should achieve something." Expectations have a sense of certainty that your young athletes will get a particular result ("We expect you to win!"). But, as I hope you understand, there is little certainty in sport where other people (e.g., teammates, competitors, coaches, officials), external factors (e.g., field, course, or court conditions, weather), equipment failure (e.g., broken bat in baseball, snapped string in tennis), and the vagaries of luck (e.g., a bad bounce, a brief distraction) can turn expectations on their head.

When you place expectations on your young athletes, you unwittingly attach a threat to them in which you connect an "or else" at the end. You might state openly or intimate indirectly, "I expect you to win today," but what your children hear is, for example, "I expect you to be win today . . . or else I will be really angry." Expectations place your young athletes, as the saying goes, "between a rock and a hard place," where they feel pressure to fulfill them or something bad will happen. As such, they come to view competition as something threatening to avoid rather than something challenging to pursue.

When Expectations and Emotions Collide

When I ask youth athletes about expectations, their reactions are pretty much the same. They frown, grimace, and get uncomfortable. They say things like, "I hate it when my parents expect things of me" and "When I build up expectations about a competition, I feel totally weighed down." Clearly these are not feel-good and play-well reactions that will benefit your young athletes.

An interesting corollary to our understanding of expectations is that they have a powerful impact on your young athletes' emotions before, during, and after competitions. They produce emotional reactions that both feel bad and usually result in poor performances. Before games, expectations produce doubt, worry, apprehension, and anxiety. During games, they cause young athletes to become distracted, tense, and tentative. They may perform tightly and cautiously, and be very self-conscious.

After the competition, if your young athletes somehow produce a good result under the weight of expectations, as alluded to earlier, their strongest emotional reaction will likely not be elation and pride, but rather simply relief because they "dodged the bullet" of unmet expectations. When your children perform poorly and don't fulfill the expectations, they will experience devastation because the expectation of experiencing success has been taken away from them.

The Wrong Types of Expectations

Many sports parents defend their use of expectations by saying, "If we don't expect things of our young athletes, they won't amount to anything." The problem is that parents often set the wrong kind of expectations. Let me clarify an important point about expectations: Not all expectations are bad. You should expect your kids to be honest, considerate, responsible, hardworking, and, appreciative. But those expectations are vastly different from expecting your children to win a game or become a professional athlete.

Expectations can be both essential tools for supporting your children's athletic efforts and potential weapons parents use against their children. Whether your expectations are beneficial or harmful to your children's athletic pursuits depends on the types of expectations you place on them.

An unfortunate mistake many sports parents make is to set expectations of which their young athletes have little or no control. An *ability* expectation is one in which children are expected to achieve a particular result based on their natural ability—"You'll win today because you're the best athlete out there." An *outcome* expectation is one in which you expect your kids to produce a certain outcome—"I know you'll get on the podium."

If your children fail to meet your ability expectations, they're forced to attribute their failure to a lack of ability—they weren't talented enough. This type of attribution is harmful because ability is not within children's control. Yes, they can become stronger and more skilled in their sport, but they are limited by the genes their parents gave them. Sadly, the failure to meet your ability expectations may cause them to come to believe they are simply incapable of being successful in the future and feel helpless to do anything about it. Your young athletes may view future success in their sport as futile and pointless. The end result is that your children won't enjoy themselves, and they are likely going to quit playing sports.

Not meeting your outcome expectations can be equally detrimental. Our society places great emphasis on competition and winning. Moreover, outcome expectations are often based on how young athletes compare to their peers— "You are a much better football player than your friend Eddie. You should definitely start ahead of him." Yet, how your kids compare to others is also not within their control. Your children may do their best but still fail to perform up to the level of their peers and fail to meet your outcome expectations. This is particularly unfair because children develop at different rates. As noted in chapter 1, children who are less successful at age 10 may catch up to and surpass their peers at age 14.

A further danger of your expressing expectations about your young athletes' ability or likely success is they will eventually internalize your unhealthy expectations. They will no longer need your expectations to feel the 50-pound weight vest. Rather, your kids will create their own unhealthy expectations. These internalized expectations shift from being about their making you happy to making themselves happy, and they will carry these unhealthy expectations into other aspects of their lives and adulthood.

Six Phrases That Put Expectations and Pressure on Your Children

You may not even realize you're placing expectations on your young athletes. You may inadvertently be putting pressure on them simply with the words you use when you discuss their athletic lives. As you can imagine, if you don't realize you're putting expectations on your children, you can't do anything to remove them.

You can place expectations unintentionally on your children by using six pressure-packed phrases when you talk to them about their sport:

- You must . . .
- You have to . . .

- You need to . . .
- You should . . .
- You better . . .
- You gotta . . .

These six phrases place a great weight on the shoulders of your young athletes, cause them to experience all kinds of unpleasant emotions, and actually interfere with their ability to perform their best and achieve their sports goals.

I suggest that you keep your radar on for the use of these six phrases; you may use them more than you think. If you see you are unwittingly including the phrases in your conversations with your children, I encourage you to replace them with six much more beneficial alternatives:

- I would like you to . . .
- I think you can . . .
- It is my goal for you to . . .
- I am working hard to help you to . . .
- I am directing my energy to support you to . . .
- I am excited to see you . . .

These six phrases have a very different feel than the previous six. Instead of threat, pressure, and anxiety, your young athletes will feel supported, positive, and fired up. And imagine how well they would perform compared to when you use the six phrases related to expectations.

> You can't live your life according to other people's expectations. If you live your life constantly trying to please others and do what they think is best for you, you will only make yourself miserable in the process. —*Corey Wayne, life coach*[14]

The Right Types of Expectations

If you want your young athletes to be successful, instead of setting ability and outcome expectations, you should establish process expectations, which they have control of and actually encourage them to do what it takes to achieve the results both you and they want. If your children feel they have your support, rather than your pressure, they are much more likely to embrace and pursue their athletic goals. Think about what your children need to do to get the results they seek and create process expectations that will lead to their success: commitment, positive attitude, hard work, discipline, patience, perseverance, and resilience. You can say, "We expect you to give your best effort" or "We expect you to stay positive and focused when you compete." Regardless of the athletic ability your children inherited from you or with whom they might be compared, they have the capacity to use process expectations and the tools associated with them to be the best they can be and find success in their sports efforts. Importantly, unlike the "or else" threat implicit at the end of an ability or outcome expectation, process expectations have an "and I'm behind you all the way" encouragement at the end.

Process expectations should be established in collaboration with your young athletes. This cooperative approach ensures that your children have buy-in of the expectations rather than feeling you have forced the expectations on them. You can talk to your children about the value of different aspects of the process in achieving their athletic goals, how it will help them achieve those goals, and that they have complete control of the process. You can share examples with your children of how notable athletes used the tools associated with process expectations to become successful. Most important, you want to help them make the connection between the process and the results of their athletic efforts.

If your children meet the process expectations, they will, in all likelihood, perform well, achieve some level of success (how successful they become will depend on what abilities they were born with), and gain satisfaction in their efforts. They will also reap the benefits of great results and recognition from their coaches and peers. And meeting the process expectations will encourage your children to set even higher process expectations. If your children don't meet the process expectations, they may not succeed and must face the consequences, including poor results and demotion in their sport. But rather than being crushed by the failure, they will know they have the power to fulfill the expectations and find success in the future.

> Fall in love with the process, and the results will come. —*Anonymous*[15]

Expectations No, Goals Yes

By now, I hope I've made it clear that establishing expectations related to ability or results will not help your children find athletic success. At the same time, as discussed previously, I recognize that results matter in sports and there's no way I can stop you or your children from talking about results. Given this reality, my intention is to allow you to speak about results in a way that will clear a path toward those results rather than building barriers that will hold them back.

The way for you to do that is to frame results in terms of goals not expectations. Goals might appear to be the same as expectations, but they are actually very different in a number of ways.

As I'm sure you know from your own athletic or career experiences, goals are deeply satisfying. When your young athletes set, pursue, and attain goals, you feel a great sense of fulfillment, as well as pride and inspiration, in seeing their efforts rewarded.

Importantly, unlike expectations, goals have two valuable benefits to your children in their athletic lives. First, instead of being either–or propositions, a key aspect of goals is that they are about degree of attainment. In other words, not every goal will be accomplished, but you can be confident that, if your children put in the requisite time and effort, they will, in most cases, show improvement and progress toward their goals. Second, goals have a very different emotional tenor for young athletes than do expectations. They breed positivity, excitement, and determination, all useful tools that will encourage your children to maintain their efforts in their sport.

Here's an example to illustrate the difference between an expectation and a goal. Let's say you inadvertently establish an expectation that your young tennis player should make the semifinals of an upcoming tournament after getting no further than the second round in previous years. Or you help your daughter set a goal of making the semifinals. She ends up losing in the quarterfinals. From the perspective of the expectation, your daughter would have failed because she didn't meet the expectation. But, with the goal, she would have been successful because she improved significantly from her previous results at this tournament by going further in the draw than she ever had.

From Outcome Goals to Process Goals

Setting outcome goals is the first step in getting away from placing expectations and pressure on your young athletes. But there's even more you can do to support and encourage them. As soon as you and your young athletes have set outcome goals, put further talk about results aside and focus on process goals, meaning what they need to do to accomplish the outcome goals. Process goals might include learning new technique or tactics, improving their fitness, or preparing their equipment.

Process goals are important for several reasons. First, unlike outcome goals, process goals are entirely within their control, so they are able to exert control on many aspects of their athletic lives to determine how well they perform. Second, if your children achieve their process goals, they are more likely to perform well, which will increase their chances of accomplishing their outcome goals.

So, what began as a misguided attempt to motivate your children with unhealthy ability and outcome expectations evolves into healthy process expectations, which mutate into outcome

> A dream written down with a date becomes a goal. A goal broken down into steps becomes a plan. A plan backed by action makes your dreams come true. —Greg S. Reid, filmmaker and author[16]

goals and then process goals, creating a virtuous cycle in which your young athletes perform well, produce their best results, and are inspired to set even higher healthy expectations and goals.

YOUR ROLE IN YOUR CHILDREN'S ATHLETIC LIVES

S imply put, you are the most powerful force in your young athletes' lives. At the same time, that power can be used in ways that help or hurt them. This chapter focuses on the different roles you play and how you can assume roles that benefit, rather than interfere with, their healthy development as athletes and people.

> At the end of the day, the most overwhelming key to a child's success is the positive involvement of parents. —*Jane D. Hull, politician and educator*[1]

YOUR NEEDS AND YOUR CHILDREN'S NEEDS

As parents, one of our most basic drives is to meet the needs of our children. Back when we were cavepeople, fulfilling our children's needs increased their chances of survival. But, moving ahead several hundred thousand years to the early part of the 21st century, most of us don't need to be overly concerned about our kids' physical survival. Yet, today, we are equally concerned about their needs in other areas of their lives, including academic, social, and, yes, athletic. We want our children to find success and happiness in whatever avenues they pursue, and most parents are willing to do whatever it takes to ensure their children grab those brass rings. And this is where things can get dicey for parents because there is a blurry line between our kids' needs and our own needs.

This distinction is crucial for several reasons. First, it influences how you think about, feel about, and act on your children's athletic lives. Second, perhaps more importantly, it will have a big impact on how your young athletes judge and respond to your involvement in their sports participation. Whether you realize it or not, your children have a very sensitive "needs radar," meaning they can perceive whose needs you are trying to meet as you expend time, energy, and money on their athletic pursuits. Your kids can sense your intentions, more specifically, whose needs you are prioritizing, whether theirs or yours. If your intentions are self-serving, they will experience them as pushing and will likely push back. If your children feel your intentions are directed toward helping them meet their needs and goals, they will experience them as support and encouragement. So, would you rather be an anchor or a sail?

Understand Your Young Athletes' Needs

Most essential to putting your young athletes' needs ahead of your own is understanding what their needs are. Perhaps the best way to judge what your children's needs are is to watch them practicing and competing. Where do they devote the most effort? What gets them excited and makes them happy? What makes them frustrated, mad, or sad? Their actions speak the loudest for what they enjoy most, what they don't like, and what their goals are in their sport.

You can also ask their coaches about your children's needs. Because they see your kids most often while in their sport, coaches are often best suited to know how your kids feel about it. This feedback is valuable because your children may behave differently when you're at practice or a game than when you're not there. You may hear about a side of your young athletes you weren't even aware of.

Finally, you can ask your children about their needs directly related to their sports participation. Particularly

> It's about getting with kids, understanding their point of view, and keeping the game simple and fun. —*Hardy Nickerson, NFL great*[2]

as your young athletes get older and become more experienced in their sport, they will have a clear idea about why they participate and what they get out of it.

Recognize Your Own Needs

Another key part of the needs equation involves recognizing your own needs in your children's athletic lives and understanding how your needs are shaping your involvement in their sports participation. What makes this process difficult is that, as human beings, we are often driven by needs of which we have little awareness, much less control. These needs may be grounded in experiences and perceptions that arose when we were children ourselves and have been reinforced for many years. For example, a father pushes his teen-aged baseball player because he never lived up to his own father's expectations when he was a young player. Or, a mother becomes overly invested in her daughter's gymnastics career because her athletic success will bolster her mother's self-esteem and feelings of self-worth. Your ability to acknowledge your needs and understand how those needs may be helping or hurting your young athletes' efforts is one of the most important things you can do to be a positive force in their sports lives.

This process of self-realization begins by "looking in the mirror" and examining what drives your involvement in your children's athletic lives. Through self-reflection or with the help of a psychotherapist, life coach, your spouse, a friend, or some other means, you can look at your needs related to your children's sports experiences that may be influencing the messages you're sending them.

A useful way to help identify any unhealthy needs that are at work is to recognize those moments when you have emotional reactions to a sports situation your children are in that seem extreme or inappropriate, for instance, anger, devastation, or hurt when they lose a competition. Ask yourself: What is the source of those emotions? What parts of you are reacting to this athletic situation in which your children are involved? What needs are driving you in your children's athletic lives?

> Children shouldn't have to sacrifice so that you can have the life you want. You make sacrifices so your children can have the life that they deserve. —Anonymous[3]

Keep Perspective

As noted in chapter 1, having a healthy perspective on your children's sports lives is one of the greatest gifts you can give them as young athletes. Because of your influence on your children, your perspective will have a big impact on the perspective they develop about their sports participation. If you have an unhealthy perspective driven by your unhealthy needs, you are setting them up for failure, ensuring they won't have a fun and life-affirming sports experience, and you are also setting yourself up for your own disappointment in their efforts.

Reality testing is an essential aspect of developing a healthy perspective. Even with the best of intentions, avoiding the Siren's call of the youth-sports in-dustrial complex can be a challenge, particularly these days when young athletes and parents alike are bombarded by messages about, as I just noted, winning, fame, and fortune through so many media outlets.

When your children show early aptitude in a sport and you fantasize about them becoming its next stars, you need a reality check. First, you should immediately return to the healthy perspective I provide in chapter 1 (you should write it down and place it on your refrigerator until your children leave for college!).

Then, as your young athletes make a greater commitment to their sport, you should regularly assess their capabilities. Unless you have experience in the sport in which your children are committed (e.g., you were an athlete or coach), you are not in a position to make accurate judgments about your children's abilities or promise. You should seek out feedback from experts who can reasonably evaluate their athletic skills.

Just because your children might not be the next great ones in their sport doesn't mean they shouldn't pursue it vigorously. If your young athletes have a great love for their sport and are determined to pursue their goals, they will reach some level of success and learn valuable life lessons that will serve them well in the future. As I told a parent of a young athlete with limited athletic ability, "Your son may not become that successful in his sport, but he will become successful at *something*."

An assessment of your children's capabilities should not be used to determine how much support and encouragement you give them. And it should never be used to set limits on their athletic dreams and goals. As someone once said, "If you don't aim for the stars, you will never even reach the top of the mountain." Rather, you should understand your children's ability so you can keep your perspective grounded in reality and focus on what you can do to offer them appropriate support.

With a healthy perspective and reasonable reality testing, you are in a position to support and encourage your young athletes in ways that will meet their needs rather than your own. Regardless of your children's ability or future promise in their sport, you will be doing what you need to do to ensure they achieve the higher level of which they are capable and gain the greatest benefits from their participation, which will serve them well in their future endeavors.

Challenge Your Child

You should do everything you can to ensure your young athletes stay interested and motivated in their sport and maintain steady progress toward their goals. Noted psychologist Mihaly Csikszentmihalyi offers an insightful way of looking at challenges in your children's athletic lives. He argues that how challenged people are depends on the relationship between the demands of the situation and the resources they have available to respond to those demands.

More specifically, in relation to youth sports, if the demands of your children's sports participation exceed the resources they have to meet those demands, they will experience frustration, lose motivation, and have decreased desire to continue their sports involvement. At the other end of the continuum, if your young athletes' resources exceed the demands of their sport, they will experience boredom and become complacent and unmotivated. According to Csikszentmihalyi, the right balance is struck when the demands of the sport slightly exceed children's ability. This relationship challenges and motivates people by enabling them to see that if they push themselves a bit beyond what they believe themselves capable of and persevere in the face of the demands of the sport, they will be successful.

You can play an essential role in helping your children find this balance. First, look at whether your young athletes appear to be bored, frustrated, or challenged. You can gauge where they are in Csikszentmihalyi's framework in several ways. You can watch them at practice and competitions, and see how they react. You can have a conversation with their coaches to get their perspective. And you can talk to your kids about their athletic experiences. From this examination, you can help them find this balance by maintaining the status quo (e.g., if it's working, keep doing it), reducing the demands (e.g., change athletic programs, move them to a lower level of competition), or increasing the resources (e.g., hire a personal trainer or pay for private coaching).

Avoid Sibling Rivalries

If you have more than one child, you will see that your young athletes' temperaments, interests, motivations, and capabilities can differ greatly. Having one child in a family who demonstrates greater interest, motivation, and ability than their siblings is common. If you lose perspective with your athletically successful child, your entire family will suffer, particularly the siblings, because they are the ones who are often left out. Putting the athletic child's needs ahead of those of siblings, who may still be finding their own interests or successes, sends a destructive message to all of your children—love and attention have to be earned by success. This message further conveys that if one of your children is less talented than another, they are not as worthy of love and their needs are less important.

To prevent this from happening, be aware of the time, attention, resources, and affection you give your children and be especially sensitive to the needs of the less-accomplished siblings. Because the athletically successful child will usually demand more attention and require more time, you need to be particularly vigilant in the distribution of your energy. Your other children are no less deserving of your love and attention, and although perhaps not yet as successful, their dreams and goals are no less important. They must be supported and encouraged for them to also gain the life lessons and benefits of whatever activities they choose and whatever level of achievement for which they strive.

Perhaps most important in your treatment of the athletic child's siblings is to help them find something for which they have passion, support their participation, and give them the time and attention necessary for them to feel loved and valued. At a practical level, this balanced approach toward your children involves giving equal time and energy to all your children in play, helping them with homework, and showing interest in all of their achievement efforts. It also means being balanced with your children in assigning responsibilities, establishing discipline, and meting out consequences without favoritism. Your goal in achieving a sibling balance is to ensure that each child feels appreciated and respected for who they are, regardless of their accomplishments.

> We are one team. . . . We work together to become better as a family and as individuals. . . . We are each others' biggest fans, supporters, and encouragers.
> —Anonymous[4]

RESPONSIBILITIES OF YOU AND YOUR YOUNG ATHLETES

Taylor's (that's me!) Law of Family Responsibilities states that if family members fulfill their own responsibilities and do not assume another's, then children have the opportunity to develop into successful and happy athletes and people; however, problems arise when parents take on the sports-related responsibilities of their young athletes and their children are not allowed to assume their own responsibilities. This usurping of responsibilities results in sport parents taking ownership of their children's athletic lives.

Your Responsibilities

Your responsibilities revolve primarily around providing your children with the opportunity, means, and support to pursue their athletic goals. Your psychological responsibilities include providing love, interest, guidance, and encouragement in their efforts. Your practical responsibilities include paying for your children's sports participation and ensuring your children have the equipment, proper instruction, and transportation, among other logistical concerns, to pursue their goals in their sport.

Your Young Athletes' Responsibilities

Your young athletes' responsibilities relate to doing what is necessary to maximize the opportunities that you give them. For example, they must be committed to their sport, give their best effort, be respectful of and pay attention to their coaches, be supportive of their teammates, stay committed, and be good sports whether they win or lose. Another essential responsibility is that they express appreciation and gratitude to you, their coaches, and anyone else who supports their efforts.

FORCED VERSUS GUIDED PARTICIPATION

The process of your children becoming athletes begins with their initial participation in a sport. Oftentimes, these first steps involve a recreational league in soccer; taking tennis, golf, or swim lessons; or throwing a baseball or football around with you in the backyard. This early involvement is so important because the quality of their initial experiences may determine their future in sports. If those first experiences aren't fun or rewarding, your children will probably lose interest and choose not to continue their participation. In contrast, if those early experiences are engaging and fulfilling, their interest will be sparked, they will be inspired to continue, and they may be the first steps to a deeper and longer-term commitment to that sport or sports in general.

You are faced with maintaining a delicate balance from the very first experiences your children have with sports. This equilibrium involves providing the impetus for them to participate long enough for them to decide whether they want to continue, yet not pushing so much that it feels coercive to them and acts to stifle their interest and motivation.

Forced Participation

Forcing your children to participate in a sport can lead to a range of problems for both them and you. Their first reaction to being forced to participate is resistance to the sport and anger and resentment toward you. You may be able to get away with forcing your children when they are young because you have significant control of them early in their lives; however, as your children grow through adolescence, pressuring them will be much less effective as they begin to assert their independence and desire to make their own choices. Additionally, some negative feelings toward parents are a natural aspect of the separation process in adolescence. But, when the negative feelings become fixated on one area, are unusually strong, and they persist, as often happens when parents strong-arm their children into playing sports, the negative emotions and damage to their attitude about sports and their relationship with you can become destructive and lasting.

Your young athletes may respond to feeling forced to participate in sports in several ways. They may resist your efforts by showing little desire or motivation in practice. They may sabotage their sports involvement by not trying, breaking their equipment, being a poor sport, not listening to their coaches, or being a bad teammate. They may even sabotage their own competitive performances by intentionally performing poorly. If you have forced your children into participating in their sport, what better way to express their resentment and resistance than by exacting revenge on you with bad behavior and poor performance.

When you pressure your children into playing sports, you not only hurt their attitude toward sports, but it can also seep into other aspects of their lives, for example, school or other avocations in which they may be involved. The negative thoughts, emotions, and behavior they experience in their sport may color their commitment to and efforts in those other parts of their lives in which you also want them to succeed. Moreover, the ill feelings they connect to their sports involvement can interfere with the possibility of future enjoyment and success in sports and beyond.

The question you may ask is: Why would any parent force their children to participate in sports? Well-intentioned reasons may include wanting to instill in children healthy attitudes and habits related to exercise and fitness; their learning important life lessons related to committing to something, setting and achieving goals, and overcoming setbacks; or keeping them so busy that they don't have time to get into trouble. Misguided reasons may include feeling

> The first thing is to love your sport. Never do it to please someone else. It has to be yours. —*Anonymous*[5]

the need to "keep up with the Joneses" in your community and wanting them to find fame and fortune as professional athletes. Truly hurtful reasons may involve driving them to find the success you didn't have as a young athlete and helping you to feel like a worthwhile parent.

Guided Participation

Raising young athletes begins with guiding your children along the path of early sports participation with the goal of leading to their fully embracing the fun and value of being athletes throughout their lives. Guided participation gives your children the support they need to overcome the many challenges of athletic involvement. It also gives them the freedom they need to choose their own path as athletes in terms of which sports they choose to participate in and the level to which they aspire.

Guided participation provides your children with the initial impetus to do sports and then, unlike forced participation, allows them to gain ownership of, motivation in, and the desire to commit to a sport. You need to strike a balance between giving your children their first exposure to experience sports in terms of direction, opportunities, and resources, and stepping back and enabling them to find their own personal connection with sports. How involved you are and how much you manage their athletic lives must shift from *direction* and *guidance* early in their sports participation to *encouragement, freedom*, and *support* as they gain experience as athletes and maturity as young people. As you can see, your involvement must decrease as time goes by. As your role decreases, the opportunity and space for your young athletes to gain increasing ownership of their sport will increase.

As mentioned earlier, your children's early participation in sports will often dictate whether they become athletes and make sports part of their lives or have a bad experience and reject sports. Because you are such a significant force in their young lives, you have the power to determine which path they take. The following are some things you can do to exert that power positively or negatively and either drive your children away from sports or draw them toward them.

Take Away the Fun

There is nothing you can do to push your children away from sports more than simply take away the fun. Nothing is more damaging to their motivation, excitement, and enjoyment than when sports become joyless, tedious, and stressful. Lack of fun is the most common reason why children lose interest in and drop out of organized sports.

Because sports are a long-term process in which its greatest rewards are not always immediate, your children need to have fun to maintain their interest and motivation. Take away the fun and your child will find few reasons to continue to participate. Sports will become work for them, a burden they feel obligated to bear, particularly if you are forcing them to participate for your own needs, not theirs.

When young athletes come to see their sports involvement as work rather than fun, it typically develops from their parents' needs, attitudes, and goals related to sports. If you force your children into participating in sports they don't enjoy or push them too much, they will lose sight of the intrinsic benefits of being an athlete and participate only for extrinsic reasons, that is, only to make you happy. This pressure from you will not only sour your children's sports experience, but also they will likely take their ill feelings toward sports out on you either directly or indirectly.

Forcing your children to participate may keep them involved in sports for a while, but the immediate and long-term consequences will be significant. In the short term, your children will be unmotivated and only expend enough effort to appease you. In the future, at the first opportunity in which you no longer have control of their participation, your children are likely to quit and find things to do that are more fun and intrinsically rewarding.

Make It Fun

You can't make sports fun. And you can't force your children to have fun in sports. Neither can fun be taught or given to them. Rather, your children must experience sports directly as young athletes and decide for themselves if they are having fun. They need to simply see that participation in sports is enjoyable and rewarding in its own right. Fun can be felt by your children in any number of ways. They may find fun in improving, being a teammate, competing, and, yes, winning.

Children are good at letting you know when they're not enjoying themselves. They demonstrate little excitement, joy, or pleasure. They don't put in much effort. They are negative about their sports participation. When you see these signs, you can assume they no longer see their athletic involvement as a positive experience. You need to explore why they aren't having fun, especially if it's a sport they had previously enjoyed. Are your children performing poorly, having conflicts with their coaches or teammates, or having other difficulties that would take away the enjoyment?

You must also look in the mirror and consider how you might be impacting their sports experience. Are you overly invested and overinvolved? Are you pushing your children too hard or inappropriately? How might you be stifling their enjoyment? As your children's most powerful role model, how you approach sports will also influence their attitude about their sports participation. If you are serious and intense, they will come to believe they better take it seriously too. You will communicate to your children that sport is work rather than play and that their involvement is serious business that isn't about fun. Conversely, if you are happy, positive, enthusiastic, and constantly talking about how fun sports are, the message you are sending your children is that sports are about fun and enjoyment, and that should be their goal.

If your children's sports participation is no longer fun because they seem to have lost interest, you will want to explore with them what has changed and see if you can reignite their interest. If they feel they are missing out on other activities in which they are more interested, you may be able to reestablish the fun by changing how much they are participating, for example, by allowing them to attend fewer practices and devote more time to the other activities. This reorganization may cause you to feel your children will no longer continue to progress in sports; however, it is better for them to develop more slowly than for them to quit and cease to participate at all. It may also be time to reevaluate their sports involvement. If your children are simply not enjoying doing sports, you should be open to the possibility that sports aren't for them and there may be other activities of equal value that will be more fun for them.

If your children are having some difficulties in the sport itself—for example, they don't like their coach or they are being bullied by teammates—you can use this opportunity to teach them about communication and resolving conflict with others. You can also speak to the coaches about the problems and enlist their help in resolving them. If these difficulties cannot be resolved and your children still enjoy the sport itself, you can consider finding another program they can join.

Your children need to find what makes sports fun for them. You can do several things to encourage fun in their sports. First, you can understand what fun means to them and find a sports experience that provides that meaning of fun for them. Second, you can clear the obstacles that cause sports to lose their enjoyment value—pressure from you, an overly competitive team, an excessively zealous coach—so that your young athletes can experience the inherent fun of sports.

A final point about sports and fun is that in reality, although sports, overall, are a really fun experience, they are also not always fun. Sports can be repetitious, monotonous, tiring, frustrating, and painful. An important lesson you can teach your young athletes is that genuine fun comes from different aspects of their sports participation and may involve different types of fun. Sometimes, the actual process of engaging in sports is fun, for instance, practicing and competing. Other times, they will find a different sort of fun in the form of fulfillment and satisfaction in the improvements they make because of their commitment and hard work. Still other times, your young athletes will find great pleasure in achieving the goals they set for themselves. Your children can also experience fun through their teammates. And, yes, there is fun to be had when they win. If you can teach your children that fun comes in many shapes and sizes, then when one aspect of their sports involvement isn't much fun (e.g., when struggling with technique or tactics, or a string of losses) and it is not much fun for a while, they can still find fun in other parts of their sports participation.

Loss of Motivation

The most obvious indicator of forced participation is a loss of motivation. Your young athletes will express their lack of motivation in several ways. They will show little sustained effort in their sport. They will give up easily in the face of minor obstacles or setbacks. Your children will be easily distracted by other activities. Overall, they will show little interest in sports and may actively sabotage their efforts and performances. The result will be a lose–lose situation; your children will have terrible sports experiences, and they will fail. Moreover, at the first opportunity, they are going to quit and find things to do that are more fun and intrinsically rewarding.

Children lose their motivation for many reasons:

- Difficult coach
- Conflict with teammates
- Lack of fun
- Slow athletic progress
- Disappointing results
- Unfulfilled goals
- Overscheduled life
- Change in goals or priorities
- Stress of school
- Family conflict

When parents first ask me to work with their children, the most common questions they ask are, "Why aren't they motivated?" and "Can you motivate them?" What parents don't realize is they are asking the wrong questions. The issue is not "Why aren't they motivated?" as if the child lacks the requisite desire and abilities to participate in sports. Rather, the question is, "What is *keeping* my children from being motivated?" in the belief that the motivation is inherent, but something—or someone—is holding it back.

I operate on the assumption that your children want to experience success and find joy in their sports involvement for one simple reason: Sports are inherently interesting and fun. Yet, your children may move in the opposite direction when they feel forced to participate. The resulting loss of motivation is often a clear sign that they are feeling coerced into participating and perceive little ownership of their athletic lives, or they aren't gaining real satisfaction from his involvement.

Regaining Motivation

A common question I'm asked by parents is: If my children lose their motivation, can it be regained? Possibly, but it can be difficult because they may already have established a strong association between their sport and feeling bad and labeled it as a bad experience. Like fun, motivation is not something you can give to your children—at least you can't give them healthy, internal motivation. Rather, they must find motivation within themselves. Whether your children can recapture their motivation will depend on the cause of its loss and what you can do to remove the obstacles that are suppressing it.

To help your young athletes regain their motivation, you must first understand why they lost it in the first place. You can ask them directly why they are no longer motivated. But to get an honest answer, your children must sense that your desire to have them resurrect their motivation is coming from a concern for their needs and goals rather than your own. You can also try an indirect route by asking more generally how things are going. You can ask what they like and dislike about their sports participation, how they are feeling about their coaches and teammates, and if there have been any problems. You should also speak to your children's coaches, who may be able to shed light on their loss of motivation. You can observe them at practices and in competitions. You might also gain some insights about the problem by speaking to the parents of their teammates who you know and who may provide some clues as to the cause of their loss of motivation in their sport.

You can also look at your involvement in your children's sports participation and consider what role you may be playing in their loss of desire. Useful questions to ask yourself include the following:

- How invested am I in my children's sport?
- What messages might I be sending that could be contributing to their decline in motivation?

- Whose needs are most being met by their continuing to participate?
- How would I feel if they quit their sport?
- What can I do to encourage and support the return of their motivation?

Your children's loss of motivation may be related directly to their sports experience or due to factors outside of their sport. You should recognize that their lives are filled with many activities and relationships that can either bolster or inhibit their motivation to participate in sports.

You can work with your young athletes to help them decide whether they should stick with their sport or choose to end their involvement and pursue another sport or activity. This decision should always be collaborative with your children to help them maintain ownership of their sport. As they consider their loss of motivation and what to do about it, you can ask some relevant questions:

- How can your current difficulties be resolved?
- If they were resolved, would you want to continue?
- What would you miss about your sport?
- What wouldn't you miss about your sport?
- What are the benefits of continuing with your sport?
- What would you do in place of your sport?
- Would you be willing to stay with your sport for a little longer to see if you can get your desire back?

Ultimately, the decision of whether your children continue should be theirs, with input from you. If the decision isn't theirs, they will fall victim to forced participation and its negative consequences. You should help your young athletes base their decision on several essential concerns:

- Is the damage done to your children's feelings about their sports participation irreparable?
- What harm could come to them if they stay in their sport?
- What lessons can they learn from continuing to participate that might produce a positive long-term outcome?
- What is the likelihood they would regain their motivation?
- Are your children willing to stick with the sport a little longer?

I cannot provide you with clearly defined guidelines for their decision. Only by carefully examining every aspect of the situation, obtaining relevant information, asking the right questions, taking a good look at your children's reactions to their sport, knowing who they are, and including them in the decision-making process will you come to the best decision.

I recommend that, instead of a decisive "I'm done!" decision, you suggest they take a break from their sport and see how they feel about it after they've been away from it for a time. I have seen many athletes who leave their sport only to find that they miss it after a few weeks or months away and return with renewed motivation. At the same time, I have seen other athletes who take a hiatus from their sport and don't miss it at all, which affirms their decision that "I'm done!" Additionally, you can tell them that the decision is not irreversible and that you and they can revisit and reevaluate it sometime in the near future to determine whether their decision is still the right one. Being loving, calm, upbeat, and supportive in this discussion can help put the decision in a positive light, show that you are there to support them, and help your young athletes make a decision that is both agonizing and relieving.

> It's important to just kind of get away from your sport until you miss it. —Misty May-Treanor, three-time Olympic beach volleyball champion[6]

Guided Participation in Action

You can get your children off on the right foot in their sports participation by taking some active steps that will set them up for great early athletic experiences. In turn, positive early sports involvement increases your children's chances that they will develop a long-term love and commitment to sports.

Exposure to Sports

Guiding your children into sports participation begins with exposing them to a wide variety of sports at an early age in the hope that one will pique their interest and, in time, encourage them to make a commitment to the sport. Parents usually first introduce their children to sports that are of interest to themselves. Perhaps parents played a particular sport when they were young or they currently engage in a sport. In both cases, parents provide their children with the awareness of and participation in a sport in which they are actively involved.

You should not, however, limit your children's exposure to sports in which you have knowledge and experience. For you to assume that what is good for you will also be good for your child is presumptuous and potentially restrictive, much as a doctor might decide that his children must also be physicians and forces them on the path to medical school. One of your great challenges is to not impose your own interests, needs, and goals on your children, but rather help them identify their own and provide the opportunities for them to nurture them.

This first step in guided participation is about being attuned to the interests of your children and letting them guide you as you guide them. This process of support will encourage them to experience many sports and find those to which they are attracted and best suited based on their talent, temperament, and interest. Providing opportunities for diverse sports experiences and allowing your children to choose their own path is a powerful demonstration of your respect for them and your desire for them to take ownership of their athletic lives.

Overscheduling

While exposing your children to many different sports is desirable, I recommend exposing them to one at a time rather than multiple sports at the same time. A ubiquitous—and unfortunate—phenomenon that has emerged in the last few decades is the overscheduling of children's lives. Today's kids are often taking music classes, playing soccer, and acting in their school play, in addition to being tutored at home and having their normal school responsibilities. If you fall prey to this overscheduling, these overly ambitious lives do more harm than good to your entire family. Your children are overwhelmed with work, feel stressed by the workload and time pressures, and have little time for free play and just being kids. This overplanned life interferes with rather than fosters their success and happiness in all aspects of their lives. With so much to do, your children have limited time to devote to or focus on any one or two activities to find out whether they actually enjoy what they are doing enough to want to commit further.

If you're like most parents these days, you are similarly overloaded trying to organize the schedules of one or more children, experience even greater stress trying to juggle these demands and "keep up with the Joneses," and have little free time to spend with your family and even less time for yourself and your spouse. You also put yourself under so much stress trying to live up to society's image of being a "good parent" that you may lose sight of what really makes parents good.

Although I can't give you definitive guidelines for how much of your children's lives should be scheduled and how much should be unstructured, I can offer a few reasonable suggestions. Your children shouldn't be involved in more than two sports or other activities at one time. They should participate in only one sport each day. Scheduling shouldn't interfere with your children's getting a good night's sleep or eating three healthy meals. Your family should be able to sit down and eat dinner together more times than not each week. Your children should be able to finish their homework well before bedtime and get to bed at a reasonable hour. They should have time at least several days a week to play outside during the day and inside in the evenings. At least several times a week, your family should have "hangout" time during which you do something—or nothing—together. Your family should share an activity at least twice a month, for instance, going for a hike, visiting a museum, or attending a concert. You and your spouse should have time to read a newspaper or a book, watch something you enjoy on television, or share a relaxed, nonchild-related conversation most evenings each week. You should have time to have dinner with friends away from your children periodically. Some of your weekends should be open and unplanned. These are general guidelines and, admittedly, may not be realistic 12 months a year. The motivation of your child, your values, and the demands of their sports will cause these guidelines to need to be modified at times. For example, many sports competitions occur every weekend during a competitive season. At the same time, most sports have offseasons that provide your young athletes and your family with the time and space to just, well, be a family.

Ultimately, you are the best judge of how much is too much. I believe that you know when enough is enough—exhausted kids, cranky parents, stressed family. Yet, it can be difficult to "just say no" when faced with a youth sports culture in which taking a weekend off marks you as a "bad parent." I encourage you to have the courage of your convictions to do what is best for your young athletes and your family rather than what other families are doing.

> We're a nation of exhausted and overstressed adults raising overscheduled children.—*Brene Brown, psychologist*[7]

And here's something that may surprise you. When you make "what's best for my family" decisions, other parents will actually be jealous of you (although they would never admit it).

Initial Impetus

Ideally, every sport you expose your children to should be one in which they are motivated to participate. Perhaps they saw a game on television or their friends participate in the sport. When your children already have the motivation to take part in a sport, my best advice is, "Get out of the way!" All you need to do is provide the necessary resources and support, and they will take care of the rest.

However, not all sports are immediately motivating. Offering your children opportunities to experience different sports sometimes means having them participate in sports in which they may not want to engage or have an instantaneous affinity for. Yet, not exposing your children to all types of sports may deprive them of finding a sport that could become their lifelong passion. You should base your decision about what sports experiences you want them exposed to on your values and interests, and what you believe might offer them enriching experiences.

In these sorts of situations, the challenge, then, is how to get your children to try a sport that they say they won't like and don't want to do. Parents often ask me, "Should I bribe my children to try a new sport?" This is a tricky question with a plethora of conflicting answers from parents, parenting experts, and researchers.

Some parents and many parenting experts swear that "bribery" is a necessary tool that parents use to motivate their children. Considerable research, however, recommends against using external rewards to bribe children to participate, indicating it actually undermines their motivation; however, this same research suggests there are some conditions in which external rewards can increase motivation. An important distinction needs to be made between immediately rewarding sports and those that are boring, difficult, or painful. Research argues strongly against providing external rewards to children for participating in sports they already enjoy. The evidence is clear that this tactic actually reduces their intrinsic motivation.

Nonetheless, using external rewards to "bribe" your child to try a sport they might not initially like can be effective. Although there are no firm rules, I can make some recommendations on how to use external rewards to your children's benefit. One reality that any parent can attest to is that children will make judgments about a sport before they have even tried it—"I know I'll hate it!"—even when they have absolutely no basis for making such a judgment. The goal of using external rewards is not to force your child to participate in a sport they know they won't enjoy. External rewards are also not aimed at providing lasting motivation to your children in a sport.

Instead, "bribes" are to offer your children some initial impetus to try a sport so they can see whether they might like it based on actual experience. I know many young athletes, including my own daughters, who swore they would hate a sport before trying it. Yet, once they did participate, they actually enjoyed it immensely and chose to commit to it of their own free will. If, in a short time, your children really enjoy the sport, you can provide the reward you agreed on because a deal is a deal. But you no longer need to bribe them because their own motivation will drive them forward. If, on the other hand, after a reasonable time of participating in the sport, your children still don't enjoy it, then, again, you provide the reward and continue to look for a sport that is a good fit for them.

The key question is what kind of external reward should you offer? The reward has to be enticing enough to motivate your children to accept the offer but not so large as to prevent them from finding their own motivation in the sport. There are no set rules here, and you should use your own judgment about what is fair and reasonable. You should start by asking your children what they think would be a good reward. Say to them, "I can see that you aren't too psyched about doing this, but we think you would enjoy it and we would like you to try it. What do you think would be a good reward for your trying it for one month?" You can solicit their ideas and then make the decision based on what you think is reasonable. Rewards should be something your children want and something you want them to have. And, hopefully, the reward will have some kind of redeeming value—which rules out junk food, video games, and expensive clothing. You should also explain the purpose of the reward and emphasize your hope that they will come to enjoy the sport on its own merits.

An important aspect of external rewards is what the reward communicates to your children. External rewards won't work if they convey incompetence, anger, lack of faith, control, or coercion (e.g., "The only way I can get you to do anything is to bribe you"). External rewards are most effective when they indicate to your children that they are valued and competent, and that you believe in them (e.g., "We love you and want to reward you for your openness and efforts"), and that you value the sport enough to want to encourage them to try it out. If external rewards are combined with love, encouragement, and praise, you are sending your children the right message and providing them with a little push so they can find out if they really like the sport.

Provide Resources

The next step in guided participation is providing the resources to ensure that your children's initial sports experiences are positive. This process involves creating a physical and psychological environment that allows your children to explore the sport fully and enables them to decide on its merits whether they wish to continue with the sport. These resources can include a youth sports program that best fits your children's interest and level of competition, and equipment, for instance, soccer shoes, tennis racquets, and baseball mitts, that will facilitate their enjoyment and success.

The youth sports program you choose to place your children in may be the most important resource you provide. A program, whether a club, team, or series of lessons, can have a big impact on the kind of experiences your children have and could determine their motivation to continue in a sport. You want to ensure that the program and its coaches share your rationale and philosophy for your children's participation and provide a positive setting in which to first expose them to a sport. You also want to ensure you enroll them in a sport for a reasonable length of time. For example, you can sign them up for a series of five tennis lessons or a six-week soccer season, enough to allow them to gauge their interest and which is not overly expensive, but not so long and expensive as to feel you wasted your money if they show no subsequent interest. Later on, if your children express continued interest, you can consider signing them up for a longer period.

As you know, some sports are equipment intensive, and the initial entry can require a substantial financial investment on your part. At the same time, the amount of the investment you make on behalf of your children should increase progressively based on the amount of their investment in the sport. A danger is that when your children show an interest in a sport, you go out and spend a lot of money on the necessary equipment and then they quickly lose interest and those purchases turned out to be a waste of money. If this occurs, it's difficult to not feel some anger toward your children and not communicate that anger. They may feel guilty and stay in the sport even though they really don't want to or become reluctant to express their interest in other sports in the future. For example, if your son shows an interest in tennis, you shouldn't go out and buy him a Roger Federer signature racquet and tennis shoes and clothing for several hundred dollars. Instead, you could buy a used racquet at a local consignment store or borrow a racquet from another family and use his old basketball shoes and some gym shoes. As his interest grows so can your investment in the equipment he needs to support his goals.

When your children begin a new sport, you should consider what resources they will need to maximize their athletic experience. Identifying potential youth sports programs and making a list of the equipment they will need will help you make deliberate choices about those resources that will allow your young athletes to explore and appreciate fully their sports experience.

Commitment

The importance of commitment is a lesson your children must learn to become successful in sports or any other part of their lives. When your children initially choose a sport in which to participate, you have an opportunity to teach them the significance of commitment as a value and a practical tool. Two of the most essential qualities associated with commitment are hard work and persistence. The reality is, if your children work hard and persist in their sport, they will likely achieve a reasonable level of competence and success.

In the early stages of your children's athletic lives, they may feel considerable frustration and discouragement as they learn its necessary rudiments. In the beginning, the costs and discomfort may outweigh the benefits and enjoyment that your children experience. This rough start may cause them to want to give up because their sports experiences are neither fun nor rewarding. You must, at this point, encourage your children to stay committed to their sport until they reach a level of competence that is fulfilling and they find it enjoyable or it becomes clear that they will never enjoy the sport.

If you allow your children to quit when their sports participation gets difficult, they won't learn the value of hard work and persistence, which are so essential to long-term success and satisfaction. Allowing your children to back out of their involvement also teaches them that they can get out of anything they don't like or that becomes difficult. It also leaves you having committed your time and money to their sport without your children's being grateful for or taking full advantage of your commitment.

Most of us remember our parents forcing us as children to do something we really did not like doing. One of two things happened: Either it became so unpleasant we stopped doing it as soon as we could—and perhaps, as adults, we are sorry we stopped—or we finally broke through the discomfort, found enjoyment and reward in it, and begrudgingly thanked our parents for keeping us committed to it.

When your children make a commitment to a sport, they must be held to it—except in the most extreme circumstances (e.g., if continued participation would do them harm)—just as they would expect you to adhere to your commitment. Imagine how your children would feel if, part of the way through a sports season that they were enjoying immensely, you decided to pull them out because you didn't feel like driving them to practice every day. They would feel disappointed and hurt. You should feel the same way and not allow your children to break their commitment either.

Commitment is not a single irreversible decision, but rather a series of increasingly more dedicated steps that lead to greater involvement in a sport. You should ask your children to make age-appropriate time commitments to the sport in which they show interest. You should establish reasonable time frames, perhaps based on a relevant period of time for the sport, for instance, a lesson package or a sports season, that you feel is adequate for them to experience the benefits of the sport. Your children should be required to stay committed for the agreed-upon time period. At the conclusion of the time commitment, you and your children can then evaluate their participation and decide whether to continue or try out another sport.

You can facilitate your children's commitment to a sport by explaining to them that commitment applies to both you and them. You can model commitment by showing your children that when they make a commitment to a sport, you also make a commitment. You should make clear to your children the commitment in terms of time, energy, and money you are making and that you expect similar commitment from them. You commit to paying for the sport; providing the necessary equipment; arranging for coaching, practice, and competitive opportunities; offering logistical support like getting them to and from practices and competitions; and giving emotional support in the form of interest and encouragement.

> The quality of a person's life is in direct proportion to their commitment to excellence. — Vince Lombardi, legendary football coach[8]

In turn, your children's commitment includes giving their best effort, paying attention to their coaches, devoting the requisite time to practicing, being considerate of their teammates, and being appropriately grateful for the opportunity you are giving them.

Goal Setting

Your young athletes can learn more about their commitment to a sport by having you assist them in setting goals for their participation. As your children become more deeply immersed in sports, goal setting acts as a guide for them as they consider the level to which they want to aspire and what they need to do to achieve that level. Goal setting is not only a useful tool to encourage commitment and hard work in sports but also a valuable tool children can learn and place in their toolbox to assist them in all aspects of their lives, throughout their lives.

Goal setting teaches your children not only where they want to go and how to get there but also essential values related to commitment and ownership. It shows them that they need to create a plan for how they will achieve their sports aspirations and then execute that plan through commitment, hard work, and patience. Goal setting helps your children understand the power of ownership of their athletic lives, in which they learn the relationship between their actions and the outcomes that result from their efforts. They learn that when they put forth effort in achieving their goals, they will usually achieve them, and when they don't, they probably won't. At an immediate and rewarding level, your children will also gain an appreciation for the meaning, satisfaction, and joy that comes from setting a goal, working hard in its pursuit, and reaching the goal. This "virtuous cycle" encourages them to continue to set and pursue goals in their sports participation.

Although a seemingly innocuous process, helping your children set goals is complicated by a number of factors. Particularly at a young age or in a sport in which they have little knowledge or experience, your children lack the perspective to set their own goals, so they must rely on you for establishing reasonable objectives related to their sports participation. In a guiding rather than a directive role, you must be careful not to impose your own needs and goals on your children. For example, if your daughter joins a soccer team, don't start thinking of her one day being in the Olympics. Goal setting is a process that begins simply and increases in detail and complexity as your children's involvement in a sport increases. In addition, from its inception, goal setting should be discussed with your children (as is age-appropriate), goals should be decided on mutually, and goals should be explicitly stated.

When your children begin participating in a sport, you should assist them in establishing three goals. The foremost goal is to have fun. Enjoying the experience is the most motivating thing for your children early in their athletic lives. If they enjoy the sport, you will have little concern for motivating them to continue to participate.

The second goal is commitment. If your children choose to participate in a sport—and you make a commitment to their involvement—your children should have a goal of staying committed for the specified duration of the sport, whether a certain number of lessons or the length of the season. This goal teaches your children the values of persistence and patience.

The third goal is to give their best effort. As I emphasize throughout *Raising Young Athletes*, one of the most important lessons your children can learn is the value of effort because that is something they can control (whereas innate talent, for example, is not) and something that is essential for athletic success, as well as success in any other avenue of life.

When your children are in the beginning stages of a sport, avoid any goal setting based on results. Outcome goals place too great an emphasis on results at too early an age and may cause your children to become preoccupied with results. And, although it is certainly fun for your children and gratifying for you to see them win, the fact is that early success isn't a good predictor of success later in their athletic lives. Everything your children do early in their sports participation involves their developing a passion for the sport, the desire to commit to and work hard in their efforts, and the willingness to learn the foundational physical and mental skills necessary for success in the years to come.

When your children are young, simply saying, "Have fun out there" or "Do your best" is not only intended as a means of expressing support and encouragement but also a statement of implicit goals for your children to strive for. As they mature (I can't give you specific ages because children develop at different rates), gain experience in their sport, and begin to have aspirations about how good they can be, you can begin to introduce a more formal understanding of goal setting with an age-appropriate dialogue about goals. This conversation should start with an explanation so they understand the concept of goals (e.g., "Goals are things you want to achieve and that you decide to work to get"). You can emphasize that goals should be within their control (e.g., "You can control whether you reach these goals by how hard you work"). Finally, you can provide examples of goals they can set and strive toward (e.g., "You can improve by paying attention to your coaches and giving your best effort at practices").

As your young athletes become more involved in a sport, goals can become more specific and more relevant to performance. The next stage of goal setting should emphasize skill acquisition and overall improvement as athletes in their sport. More specifically, your young athletes' goals should focus on their getting better technically and tactically, and translating that progress into improved overall performance. Importantly, only when your children make a long-term and time-intensive commitment to their sport and choose to pursue it to the fullest of their abilities should outcome goals become part of their goal setting.

You should recognize your own limitations in assisting your children in setting outcome and long-term goals. Unless you have in-depth knowledge of the sport, gained either as an athlete or coach, you can do more harm than good by trying to set goals for them. The wise course at this point is to seek out your kids' coaches, who can provide experienced guidance about reasonable goals for your children to set based on their current level of performance and the developmental trajectory they are on.

To help you better understand goal setting so you can more effectively guide your children in setting goals, the following are a few criteria you should follow, based on the S.M.A.R.T.E.R. model.

The acronym S.M.A.R.T.E.R. represents the five criteria research has found you can use to get the most out of your goal setting (note that there are variations on what each letter in the acronym stands for, and I have chosen those I think are most effective).

Specific. Your goals should be specific to what you want to accomplish. For example, if you are a lacrosse player, you wouldn't want a general goal like, "I want to improve my stick handling." Instead, you want to identify what aspects of your stick handling you want to get better at. A more appropriate goal might be, "I want to improve my passing accuracy just outside the crease." The more specific you can get, the more you can focus on what you need to do in your training to improve that area.

Measurable. You want your children's goals to be objective and measurable. For example, if you have a child who is a tennis player, a measurable goal might be, "I want to improve my first-serve percentage from 45 percent to 65 percent in tournament matches." This goal identifies the target your children can aim for. Next, you want to establish a process goal that will lead to that improvement goal. Continuing the tennis example, a good goal might be, "My goal is to hit 50 serves three times a week for the next four weeks to raise my first-serve percentage."

Accepted. As discussed in chapter 1, ownership of your children's sport is essential for their athletic success. Ownership is also relevant to the goals your young athletes set for themselves. Goals that are set by you or their coaches will not fully inspire or motivate them because they don't come from your children themselves, so they won't have full ownership of them. When your children set goals for themselves (with guidance, if necessary from you or their coaches), achieving those goals will be grounded in their determination and drive to be the best athletes they can be. Because they own their goals, they can't not give their best effort as they strive toward them.

Realistic. For goals to support rather than discourage your young athletes' efforts, they must be realistic but also a bit of a stretch. If they set goals that are too easy to achieve, your children will have no incentive to work hard to achieve them because they'll reach their goals with little effort. Conversely, if they set goals that are too impossible to attain, they will realize there is little point in expending effort toward those goals because they can't reach them anyway. You want your children to set goals that are attainable, but only with hard work and pushing their limits.

Time limited. Research has shown that the most effective goals have a time limit set for them. In other words, you would help your young athletes to establish goals with a particular deadline for accomplishing them. These time limits act to motivate your children to exert effort consistently in pursuit of their goals to ensure attainment within the desired time frame. For example, if your son is a golfer who wants to improve his putting accuracy, a time-limited goal might be, "I'm going to practice my putting (one bucket of 50 balls) three times a week with the goal of lowering my handicap by two strokes within the next eight weeks."

Exciting. Emotions lie at the heart of your young athletes' motivation. If they are excited about their sport, they're going to work hard. As a result, you want to help your children set goals that inspire and excite them. Their emotions are so important because they can have a big influence on your kids' efforts and whether they attain their goals when faced with failures, disappointment, fatigue, pain, tedium, and the desire to do other things. As your children set goals, ask them whether the goals pass the "excitement" test, that is, do the goals get them fired up to achieve them?

Recorded. Considerable research has demonstrated that your young athletes will stay more committed to their goals when they write them down than if they just think about them. Recording goals seems to help in several ways. First, the physical act of writing appears to make the goals more tangible and real. Second, the act of writing goals down seems to create a sense of ownership that makes the goals feel more like theirs, compelling children to commit to them. Fourth, posting the written goals where your kids can see them regularly acts as a constant reminder of what they want to achieve and what they need to do to attain them. Finally, another research finding is that your young athletes will be more committed to their goals if they make them public by sharing them with family, friends, and, these days, social media. Making the goals a public declaration appears to generate a stronger sense of accountability, which creates positive pressure on children to adhere to the goals.

In addition to the S.M.A.R.T.E.R. goals I just described, there are two things you can help your young athletes do in their goal setting. First, their focus in their goal setting should be on the degree of attainment rather than absolute attainment. An inevitable part of goal setting is that your children won't reach all of their goals because it's not possible to accurately judge how realistic all goals are. If your children are concerned only with whether they reach a goal, they may see themselves as failures if they are unable to do so. This disappointment will invariably reduce rather than bolster their motivation. You should empha-size how much of the goal your children achieved rather than whether the goal was fully realized. Although your children won't attain all of their goals, they will almost always improve toward a goal. With this perspective, if your kids don't fully reach a goal but still improve 50 percent from the previous level, they will still see themselves as having been successful and their commitment and effort will be rewarded. For example, a cross-country-running daughter's goal is to finish in the top 10 of an upcoming race after having only finished as high as 18th in previous races. But she finished 12th in her next race. Even though she didn't reach her goal of a top-10 finish, she did improve from 18th to 12th, which should still be a "win" for her.

Also, you should ensure that your young athletes receive consistent feedback about their goals. This information serves several purposes. It keeps your children focused on their goals, so they maintain their commitment in their pursuit of their goals. Feedback shows progress toward your kids' goals, rewarding their efforts. It also emphasizes the relationship between effort and achievement by connecting their goals, and the effort they put into them, with improvement. Feedback can come from you, from your children's coaches, from themselves, or directly from successful experiences.

> The real value of setting goals is not the recognition or reward, it's the person we become by finding the discipline, courage, and commitment to achieve them. — Cat Smiley, fitness expert[9]

Ongoing Encouragement

As your young athletes increasingly immerse themselves in a sport, ongoing encouragement is a valuable gift you can give them. When most people think of encouragement, what comes to mind are such platitudinous comments as, "Nice job" or "Way to go." Real encouragement, however, is much more substantial and purposeful. Being conscious of what you're communicating to your children can have a significant impact on their perspectives, attitudes, and reactions to their sports participation.

Meaningful encouragement serves many roles. It acts to focus attention on important values you want your children to get from their athletic lives. For example, simple encouragement like, "You really stuck with it in really tough conditions today" and "You were a great teammate in today's game" clearly communicate the value of perseverance and teamwork, respectively, which are necessary for your children to become successful in sports, as well as in other aspects of their lives.

Substantial encouragement also reinforces why your children are participating. Support that emphasizes fun ("You looked like you were having a great time"), mastery ("You are improving so much"), cooperation ("It's great to work as a team, isn't it?"), and competition ("It is so exciting to compete and do your best") further facilitate the internalization of ownership in your children's athletic lives.

Proper encouragement keeps the focus on your young athletes' understanding that the achievement is truly theirs, rather than external validation from you. When your children do something well, you are actually not helping when you say things like, "We are so proud of you," "We love you so much," or "You deserve a reward," as nice as they might seem. However well-intentioned, focusing on how you feel, expressions of love, or providing material rewards for success mistakenly link your children's efforts and successes with external sources of validation, for instance, your love and material inducements. Instead, you want to connect their efforts and

> Behind every young child who believes in himself is a parent who believed first. —*Matthew L. Jacobson, motivational speaker*[10]

accomplishments with the internal benefits of participation, for example, fun, mastery, achieving goals, and social interaction. Good examples are as follows: "You really stuck with your game plan even when you were behind. That took guts!" And also, "You must feel so proud of your efforts in today's game."

Freedom

Freedom is the culmination of your and your young athletes' journey into the sports world. Your efforts early in your children's athletic lives are aimed at instilling in them the attitudes and skills they will need to find enjoyment, fulfillment, and success as they mature as athletes and people. At the appropriate time, you must trust that you have laid the foundation so you can step back from your children's athletic achievements, both literally and figuratively—just as you will do as they make the transition into adulthood—and enable them to take full ownership of their athletic lives and find their own path in sports. Your role will shift from control and management early in their athletic lives to guidance and support later on. This means letting your children experience both success and failure, joy and pain, and giving them the opportunity to come to terms with these experiences and use them to grow. Only by offering this freedom can you ensure that your children gain full ownership of their sports participation and build a deep and personal relationship with their sport. As your children mature as athletes and people, and gain experience in their sport, you want them to build on their own passion for the sport, their own deeply felt joy in its experience, and the self-generated rewards of participation and accomplishment in their sport.

Giving your young athletes the freedom to fully own their athletic lives does not mean letting them go completely. A strong connection between you and your children in their sports participation is essential as they expand their boundaries because it provides a safety line as they explore their athletic lives and a secure haven to which they can return when the seas of sport get rough. Also, your children's sports participation is a wonderful opportunity for you and your children to share their experiences and growth. So, giving your children this freedom actually strengthens your connection.

Your Children's Choice

Almost every young athlete I see in my work wants to be successful. Many want to attain lofty sports goals, whether it be as collegiate, Olympic, or professional athletes. But, realistically, few will attain such grand heights in sports. That, however, doesn't make the journey any less meaningful or satisfying. Ultimately, you want your young athletes to pursue their own personal greatness, however high up the competitive ladder that may take them. You want your children to define success in terms of the commitment and effort they put into and the joy and fulfillment they get out of their sports experiences, and the essential life lessons that they garner from their sports participation that can serve them well in all aspects of their lives, throughout their lives.

At the end of the guided participation process I have just described, if you embrace a healthy and supportive role in your children's athletic lives, you will give them and yourself two wonderful gifts. First, you will lay the foundation for an incredibly positive and impactful sports experience that will pay immediate and long-term dividends in many areas of their lives. Second, you will build a strong and resilient bond with

> To raise a child who is comfortable enough to leave you, means you've done your job. They are not ours to keep, but to teach them to soar on their own. —Anonymous[11]

your children that will include and transcend their athletic lives, and create a relationship of love, support, and guidance that will last for many years to come.

SEND THE RIGHT
MESSAGES TO YOUR
YOUNG ATHLETES

A question that fascinates me as both a so-called sport parenting expert and the father of two young athletes is: How do children become who they become, or, in the context of sports, how do young athletes become who they become? As noted previously, genetics play an essential role in how athletes develop; height, body type, inborn talent, and temperament have a strong hereditary component in terms of how far they go in their sport and how much they enjoy their athletic experiences. As legendary basketball coach Red Auerbach once said, "You can't teach height." Yet, evidence is equally strong that environment also contributes significantly to how successful athletes become. If athletes don't also develop the right attitude and commit Herculean effort in their athletic pursuits, those inborn qualities will only take them so far. The old nature versus nurture argument has been rendered obsolete; it is now a widely accepted belief among sports experts that both nature and nurture play a substantial role in athletic development.

Although genetics have a big impact on how your young athletes develop, I don't like to talk about it much for one simple reason: Your children can't do anything about the genes you gave them. If they were lucky enough to win the "athletic gene lottery," good for them, as they get a head start on everyone else, but, given that the world is full of athletically gifted failures (because they didn't do the work to fully realize their talents), it doesn't offer them a sure path to sports success. If they received less athletic genes from you, well, that is a bummer, but it doesn't necessarily doom them to sports failure. Rather, they'll just have to leverage other influences on athletic performance that are within their control, including smarts, confidence, focus, intensity, and just plain old determination, to become as good an athlete as they can be.

So what aspects of environment impact children's athletic development? Some have argued that parents have much less influence than they like to think; peers and the prevailing youth sports culture affect children more; however, I believe that, particularly during the early years of children's athletic lives, you have a window of opportunity to have a greater impact on them before they become fully integrated into the larger athletic world.

Consider this: Parents are the most present people in their children's early lives and exert the most control over almost everything your children experience, both within and outside of their sports participation. Whether it is what they eat, when they sleep, their daily activities, or with whom they interact, you are in charge. During this period, you provide your children with most of their developmental "nourishment" in the form of words, emotions, behavior, and interactions. And, importantly, you create the physical and social environment that plays an increasingly important role in your children's later development as athletes and people, including your home, the neighborhood in which they live, the schools they attend, the sports they engage in, the teams they join, the peers with whom they interact, and the types and frequency of exposure they have to the youth sports culture and the larger popular culture. In other words, especially during those early years, you have the opportunity to control the messages your children get.

> Some people have to wait their entire lives to meet their favorite athlete. I raised mine!—*Anonymous*[1]

MESSAGES MATTER

Perhaps the most powerful lesson I have learned as a "parenting expert" and father about the role of nurture in the development of children and, by extension, young athletes, is that *young athletes become the messages they get the most.* The messages they receive, whether from you, their teammates, their coaches, or the youth sports culture, will dictate their attitudes about themselves as young athletes, which will also act as a lens through which they view their sports experiences. Both will—in turn—significantly influence your children's emotional experiences in their sport; their interactions with teammates, coaches, and competitors; and how they perform in competitions.

Given the importance of your controlling the messaging your children get about their sports lives and the inherent power you have in shaping your children and their athletic experiences through your messages, the core question you should ask yourself is, How can I be sure I'm sending the healthiest messages to my young athletes? The answer to that question has two parts. First, you need to be clear about what messages you want to communicate to your children. And, second, you must develop your own skills in conveying those messages.

These messages that come early in your children's athletic lives are particularly significant because, before long, they will be getting messages from many much less controllable and benign sources. Teammates, coaches, and the broader youth sports culture will inexorably send your young athletes all kinds of messages, some good and some downright unhealthy. All you can do is attempt to ingrain positive messages early in your children's lives as a form of immunization against the onslaught of harmful messages they are certain to receive as they get older and immerse themselves more deeply in sports.

> I don't know any other way to lead but by example. — *Don Shula, former NFL coach*[2]

MESSAGES FROM THE YOUTH SPORTS CULTURE

Our youth sports culture has certainly changed during the past quarter-century. In decades past, youth sports were about fun, kids being active, enjoying competition, and developing healthy life skills and habits. And, to be fair, some of that still exists in some parts of the youth sports culture. At the same time, we have seen a sea change in the goals and focus of youth sports. These changes have occurred for several reasons. First, they are due to shifts in the economics of sports in which sports are now big business. Along with this change, professional and Olympic athletes can now earn millions of dollars in salaries, prize money, and product endorsements. These riches can act as a Siren's call to parents who believe their young athletes can reach those heights.

Along with sports becoming a big business, they have also joined the ranks of big entertainment, in which televised sports, including professional, Olympic, and collegiate competition, earn billions of dollars for leagues, teams, universities, and other sports organizations. Add radio broadcasts, printed sports magazines, and, in the past 15 years, the rise of the internet, and athletes, even at a young age, can attain levels of fame that were unheard of 25 years ago.

With the stakes so high, the old values, goals, and messages associated with youth sports have been supplanted by those that, as I mention earlier in *Raising Young Athletes*, better meet the needs of adults rather than children, from private sports coaches to sports agents to college and professional teams to youth sports organizations to sport parents themselves. These changes have, not surprisingly, led to substantive changes in the messages being sent to young athletes from the groups I just referred to. Although there are still many healthy messages emanating from our youth sports culture, sadly, unhealthy messages may outweigh the healthy ones in frequency, strength, and attractiveness. Examples of these harmful messages include the following:

- Self above team
- Early success matters
- Winning is the only thing
- Fame and fortune
- Excessive celebration
- Fighting
- Cheating
- Drug use
- Violence

These messages from powerful forces are those you must battle against every day as your children enter and immerse themselves in sports. As a consequence, you need to gain a deep understanding of messaging and develop effective messaging tools for you to resist these ever-present messages and ensure you expose your children to the healthiest messages possible as their athletic lives develop.

> Sport is born clean, and it would stay that way if it was the athletes who ran it for the pleasure of taking part, but then the fans and the media intervene and finish up by corrupting it with the pressure that they exercise. —*Bode Miller, U.S. ski racing Olympic gold medalist*[3]

Types of Messages

As I discuss in the introduction, value messages are the foundation of the messages you send your young athletes and the messages they receive from you and the broader sports culture because the values they adopt will act as the signposts for who they become and the direction their lives take. The value messages your children internalize early become what they deem important as they develop as athletes. For example, if you send them the message that sports are all about winning early and often, that attitude will guide how they approach their athletic lives in the future, with obvious repercussions described earlier in the book. By contrast, if your messages emphasize fun, effort, teamwork, and being a good sport, your young athletes will view their sports participation through the lenses of those values.

Unfortunately, once your children leave the nest of home, many of the values to which they are exposed in their athletic lives will not be healthy ones. Given all of the bad value messages young athletes are getting from our current sports culture, whether cheating, drug use, grandstanding, or violence, it is an immense challenge for parents to stem that tide and instill healthy values in them. If you can inculcate positive sports values through good messages early in your children's athletic lives, you'll be ingraining healthy values that will be more impervious to the unhealthy values with which they will be confronted once they enter the larger social (and digital) world of sports.

Attitude messages your children receive about themselves early in their sports involvement, for example, confidence, perseverance, healthy risk taking, and patience, will become internalized when faced with the inevitable challenges in different aspects of their athletic life, for instance, in practice or during important competitions. These attitude messages are initially created through your relationship with your young athletes, your attitude toward their sports participation, and the messages you send them about your attitude toward them.

Messages related to the physical health benefits of sports can be some of the most enduring messages you send them. In a modern world in which unhealthy physical habits dominate the landscape, including bad nutrition, excessive use of technology, poor sleep habits, a sedentary lifestyle, and obesity, early messages supporting the value of sports can mitigate the cultural messages they are certain to receive and set them up for a life of physical health and vitality.

Messages that your young athletes receive related to the social and relationship aspects of sports can also shape their future lives both within and outside of sports. Messages of camaraderie, cooperation, and team goals, for example, can help your children experience success and satisfaction in their team sports involvement, as well as in their education, careers, and personal lives that lie ahead.

How Messages Get Sent

Your children's attitudes about their sports participation develop from several message sources. Role modeling from you, teammates, coaches, and other visible people in their athletic lives provides young athletes with their earliest messaging. When your children see influential people in their sports involvement—and you are, by far, the most important person in their athletic lives—act a certain way in various situations, they come to internalize those messages.

For example, if your young baseball player sees a MLB star arguing with an umpire about a perceived bad call, the message your child gets is that it's okay to challenge calls at the plate and disrespect the umpire. You can see the power of this role-modeling effect in simple ways, for instance, the body language and vocabulary your children pick up from you, teammates, coaches, or watching top athletes in their sport on television.

Once your children fully develop language skills, you can send messages directly through discussions of appropriate behavior in situations and conversations following teachable moments. Ultimately, positive messages are instilled through sheer repetition; the more your young athletes see and hear the same healthy messages, the more deeply ingrained those messages will become and the more likely those messages will be internalized as healthy attitudes, emotions, behavior, interactions, and performance in their sports participation.

> I don't believe professional athletes should be role models. I believe parents should be role models. It's not like it was when I was growing up. My mom and my grandmother told me how it was going to be. If I didn't like it, they said, "Don't let the door hit you in the ass on your way out." Parents have to take better control. — *Charles Barkley, former NBA player*[4]

No Guarantees, But . . .

Even if your young athletes are bombarded with messages about healthy values, attitudes, physical health, and relationships early in their athletic lives, it doesn't guarantee they will stick forever. As your children move into the bigger sports world, the messages they will receive that contradict your own will grow in frequency and intensity. This means that your job of healthy messaging never ends. In fact, it may be more important as your children develop as athletes and pursue increasingly higher goals. As they progress up the competitive ladder, you must continue to send positive messages, protect them as much as you can from bad messages, and help them to make good choices about the messages they see, hear, and experience.

Send Messages to Yourself Too

The notion of messages doesn't just apply to your young athletes. They can also play a big role in how you parent them as they enter and engage more deeply in their sports. Your young athletes aren't the only ones in your family who are vulnerable to unhealthy messages. You too are exposed to many messages from other parents; the teams your children play on; and the larger sports culture that you see, hear, and read about through many media. As a human being, you will feel pressure from these messages that, for example, "winning is everything" and you have to "keep up with the Joneses." These messages are difficult to resist because you are surrounded by them; and many parents around you have fallen prey to their unhealthy messages as well. You may begin to, without realizing it, internalize those bad messages and communicate them to your children.

Herein lie the real benefits of early positive messaging for both your young athletes and you. In the early stages of your own parenting, you send a variety of messages to your children and communicate them in different ways. You are not only conveying those messages to your children but also sending them to yourself. In doing so, you receive the very messages intended for your children and, as a result, ingrain them in yourself.

This unintentional self-messaging is so important because when you send healthy messages early in your children's athletic lives and, in doing so, fully embrace those messages yourself, you prepare yourself to resist the equally seductive, yet unhealthy, messages you as a sport parent are also vulnerable to and will likely face as your children immerse themselves in their athletic lives. Moreover, as you become a skilled messenger when your children are young, you'll be better able to use those messaging skills later in their athletic lives when, as already noted, you will need them even more. When you instill positive messages in yourself and your children, you gird yourself and them against the often-toxic messages both of you will surely receive as your children get older and become more involved in sports.

> Little League Baseball is a very good thing because it keeps the parents off the streets. — *Yogi Berra, baseball legend*[5]

Create Your Children's Athletic World

When your children enter the youth sports world, about the same time as they first attend school, they are entering a wide world in which others can, for the first time, exert an influence that is potentially greater than your own. As soon as your young athletes walk out your front door and onto their sport's field of play, they are receiving messages of all sorts from their immediate athletic world, including from teammates, coaches, and other parents. This social world can be an immense source of messages because you can't control everyone or everything to which your children are exposed outside of your home.

You can't fully shield your young athletes from the messages they receive from the sports world, but you can do your best to minimize their exposure to messages you don't want them to get for as long as possible. The best way to do this is to thoughtfully create a sports world that will communicate the messages you want them to receive. You can accomplish this in several ways. First, expose your children to sports you believe will offer them the most benefit. For example, you might believe endurance sports or technical sports will help them the most. Second, help your children to choose a sport that will be the most fun and motivating based on their capabilities and interests. Third, find a sports program that is consistent with your values and goals for their sports participation. Fourth, within the sports program you and your children choose, seek out like-minded parents who will send messages that are aligned with your own. From the relationships you build with families with similar values, interests, and goals for sports participation, your children will develop friendships with peers who are also compatible. The end result is an athletic world that, at least at the local level, is sending messages that are positive, healthy, and consistent with your own.

How to Send the Healthiest Messages to Your Children

I hope I've convinced you of the importance of messaging to your children in their athletic lives. This effort on my part leads to an essential question to ask yourself: How can I be sure I'm sending the healthiest messages to my young athletes? There are steps you can take to come up with the correct answer.

First, know what messages you want to send to your children. As you expose your children to the sports world, you should be thoughtful and deliberate about why you want them to participate in sports, the kinds of experiences you want them to have, and what you want them to get out of their athletic lives. Returning to the four types of messages detailed earlier in this chapter, what types of messages related to values, attitudes, physical health, and relationships do you want them to receive from their sports involvement?

Second, take a long, hard look in the mirror and see what messages you actually do send to your young athletes. Let's be realistic. We typically know what is best for our children, but, as human beings, we also have to admit we don't always do what's best for them. Although a decidedly uncomfortable process, this period of self-reflection is essential for ensuring you're communicating the best messages to your children. Reasons for your communicating unhealthy messages to your children about their sports participation may be due to experiences you had as an athlete in your youth; messages about sports ingrained by your parents; having been seduced by the messages of our youth sports culture; or your own "baggage" (we all have it), which might be comprised of unfulfilled sports dreams, self-doubt, insecurities, or fear of being a bad parent.

Third, now that you have a deep understanding of the messages you want to convey to your young athletes and also acknowledge the messages you do send them, your next task is to ensure that your desired messaging is aligned with your actual messaging. If the messages are, great, you can move forward in your messaging. But, if they aren't, you need to hit the pause button and come to understand why the disconnect exists and how you can connect them.

Fourth, you need to develop effective messaging skills to send the most positive messages to your young athletes and ensure that they receive them as intended, maximizing the messages' impact on your children. Later in this chapter, I describe a number of message "conduits" you can use to send messages.

Finally, in addition to consistently sending healthy messages about your children's sports experience, you have to do everything you can to ensure that those messages actually get through to your children loud and clear. To that end, you need to understand what message "blockers" might be preventing them from getting your messages, which I will discuss later in this chapter.

> Teaching kids to count is fine, but teaching them what counts is best. —*Bob Talbert, politician*[6]

Key Messages to Send Your Young Athletes

Although there are many positive messages you can communicate to your young athletes about their sports participation, there are several core messages that should act as the foundation for your messaging.

- Have fun.
- Give your best effort.
- Be a good sport.
- Support your teammates.
- Listen to your coaches.
- Mistakes and failure are actually good.
- If you win, it's icing on the cake.
- We love you!

If you send these messages to your children early and often, they will develop healthy values, attitudes, and habits related to their athletic lives that will serve them well as they deepen their relationship with sports and in their lives outside of sports.

You can communicate these messages in several ways that will help them get the messages and convey a "meta-message" that you are there for them in their athletic lives. These meta-messages can include the following:

- Expressing love and affection
- Helping set reasonable goals
- Tangibly supporting their efforts (e.g., paying for their sports participation, buying them the necessary equipment, getting them to practice, attending competitions)
- Providing regular encouragement
- Staying calm during competitions
- Being positive after failures
- Offering a healthy perspective about the importance of sports in their lives

Your Young Athletes Send You Messages Too

While my focus in this chapter has been on how you can send healthy messages to your young athletes, the message highway is not one way. Your children are constantly sending you messages you may or may not be getting or interpreting correctly. Your ability to receive and understand those messages can, in turn, help you send the best messages in the best way (and help you know when to stop sending or change your messages).

Your children are incredibly good at sending you messages about how they are doing at any given moment in time in their sports participation. Unfortunately, we aren't always great at interpreting them. For example, when your young athletes don't feel like practicing their sport, you may interpret that message as meaning they've lost their motivation or, even worse, are being lazy. Yet, the real message may be that they are just tired and need a break to recharge their batteries. These are very different interpretations that will produce very different reactions on your part.

Your young athletes will also tell you how well your messages are getting through to them. You can judge the effectiveness of your "message transmission" by seeing whether their words, emotions, behavior, interactions, and performances are consistent with your messages. For example, if they continue to compete hard when they're behind in a game, congratulate their opponents after a loss, and thank their coaches after every practice, then you are getting a pretty clear message that they are getting your messages about perseverance, being a good sport, and expressing gratitude toward those who make their sports participation possible. If they aren't affirming your messages and are, in fact, sending contradictory messages, that is another powerful message in itself, namely, that you are either inadvertently sending the wrong messages or, for some reason, something is blocking your messages from getting through, they are not understanding the messages as intended, something is motivating them to act counter to the messages, or they just haven't gotten your message enough. You can use this information to figure out how to alter your messages so they will get through and have the desired effect.

Your young athletes will often send you a message that it is time to change your message. Think about it this way: The point of sending messages is to get into their heads. But when you get into their heads too much with the same message, it can get crowded and feel overwhelming, and that is really annoying for children. In fact, when I work with young athletes, I know they are getting my messages when they give me a look that says, "Okay, I get it!" or they tell me outright that I'm really irritating them. So, I get their message and back off or send a different message. Their messages may be ones of "enough!" but the larger message is, "I got the message, thank you, you don't need to keep sending it!"

MESSAGE CONDUITS AND MESSAGE BLOCKERS

Message Conduits

Now that you understand the importance of sending positive messages to your children related to their sports participation, a key question you should ask yourself is: So how do I get healthy messages across to my young athletes? Before you can take actual steps to communicate specific messages, let me explain the various "conduits" through which you convey messages to them.

What You Say

Your messages come from what you say to your young athletes directly. For example, "You stayed really focused after you let that goal in!" or "You were a really good sport for congratulating your opponent after you lost." Before you communicate an important message to your children, be sure to consider what the real message you want to convey is and if your words will best convey that message. For instance, a key message I believe your young athletes should get early and often from you is to give their best effort and never give up no matter what. Yet, in response to their children demonstrating persistence, many parents say something like, "Good job out there!" What message does this impart? The message is that they did a good job, which, I'm sure you would agree, is a pretty vague message because it isn't clear what they did that made it a good job.

The purpose of messages is to encourage and reinforce values, attitudes, behaviors, interactions, and performances you want them to ingrain and repeat in their athletic lives. If you want your young athletes to ingrain the value of persistence and persevere in practice and competitions, a better message might be, "You kept trying your hardest even when you were behind!"

Be aware, however, that verbal messages have their limits. With younger children, their not-yet fully developed language skills may prevent them from understanding your messages. For older athletes, their emotional state at the moment of your messaging may interfere with the message getting through. For all young athletes, the messages you send through your emotions and actions (to be discussed later) that contradict your verbal messages may prevent your spoken messages from getting through.

What You Feel

You send messages to your young athletes about your feelings toward their sports participation in the emotions you express through your tone of voice, facial expressions, and body language. In fact, your emotional messages may be the most powerful because children, as verbal beings who are not yet fully developed, are highly attuned to their parents' emotions. Make no mistake about it, your children will pick up your emotional messages more quickly and more impactfully than any other message. If you are angry after a loss, they will get that message, no matter how you try to suppress it. If you are happy after a win, they will feel it too, no matter what you say. Even if you say or do something in an attempt to counter or cover up your emotions, your emotions will be louder than your words or actions and will take precedence in the psyches of your young athletes. And, particularly for younger athletes, you can say something and, while they may not completely understand the words, if the message is infused with the appropriate emotional content that is consistent with the verbal message, they will get the deeper message.

What You Do

The cliché "actions speak louder than words" is as true with children, if not truer, as with anyone else. Young children are incredibly alert to what you do. They are watching and listening even when you don't think they are. For example, after a game, they comment about your reaction on the sideline while they were on the field. I'm sure you've been in a situation in which your children mimic your facial expressions, body language, words, and behavior without even realizing you express yourself in those ways. Put simply, your children want to do what you do. That influence bestows on you extraordinary power as a role model. But, as the saying goes, with great power comes great responsibility. Yes, this realization might instill in you great fear that your children might pick up some of your less-admirable messages. At the same time, you also possess the ability to model wonderfully positive behavior related to their sports participation.

Because of your influence as a role model, you should be ever vigilant about the messages that your actions communicate to your young athletes. Particularly in the sports arena, your behavior will be especially influential. Your actions at your children's practices and competitions send messages that can be positive or negative. For example, if you are constantly talking to their coach, trying to be an "arm chair" coach at home (particularly if you don't have any experience in their sport), or yelling at the refs or umpires, your actions are sending unhealthy messages to your children. Conversely, if you are present, but quiet, at practices and cheering for both teams at games, your behavior conveys healthy messages.

If you're also an athlete who trains and competes, your behavior in this role, so similar to what your young athletes are doing, can send even more powerful messages. The passion and enjoyment you express when engaging in your sport, the time and effort you put into the pursuit of your goals, how you react to challenges and setbacks, and the way you respond to successes and failures send clear messages your children will emulate in their own athletic lives.

Who You Are

When I talk about communicating messages to your young athletes through your words, emotions, and actions, I don't just mean the messages aimed specifically at them for their particular consumption. In fact, the messages you send to them inadvertently by just being who you are, that is, the way you are in your daily life and the ways in which you interact with the sports world and beyond, may have an equally influential effect on them. Your relationships with others in your life; your career, avocations, and interests; and your conversations with others during which your children are within earshot convey powerful messages to your children that can impact their athletic lives.

This influence of who you are on your children can be two sides of the same coin when it comes to the messages you send them by just being you. The positive side of the coin is shiny and smooth, from which you have the ability to convey really wonderful messages. For instance, if you express your love for your children before and after competitions, stay calm after a painful loss, and congratulate the parents of the winning team, you send your children really healthy messages.

The other side of the coin, however, is more tarnished and rough. One thing people often forget, as mentioned earlier in this book, is that parents are, first and foremost, human beings who bring to their role as parents lots of good stuff but also likely some baggage from their upbringing that can prevent them from sending the most positive messages to their children. These less-than-healthy messages are also expressed in the totality of who you are: how you describe the world, the emotions that dominate your life, the behavior in which you engage in your daily activities, and the interactions you have with people. For example, if you are judgmental toward others, yell when angry, or treat your siblings badly, you are sending decidedly unhealthy messages to your children. Your goal (and challenge) is to highlight and communicate the positive aspects of who you are and be aware of and mitigate the less-attractive qualities you, like all parents, possess.

The messages you send to your children not only influence how their minds work but also produce neurological changes in the structure and functioning of the brain. Recent research suggests the presence of a "mirror neuron system," a part of the brain that is activated when children observe others, particularly those they deem important to them. It is believed to be associated with essential personal and social functions, including empathy, nonverbal communication, emotional recognition, social behavior, motor skills, and language. This neurological effect further highlights the importance of your messaging because it indicates that your messages become "hardwired" into your children's brains, making them both enduring and difficult to change.

What Your Children Do

Your actions speak louder than your words in your children's sports participation, but your young athletes' own actions speak even louder. What this means is that the more you can get your children to engage in words, emotions, and actions that represent the messages you want to communicate, the more directly and powerfully they will ingrain and adopt those messages as their own. In other words, when your children talk, feel, or act in ways in their sport that convey a message, for instance, "I'm going to keep fighting even if I fall behind in my match," "I'm really excited about playing in the finals today," or "I'm going to really support my teammates in tomorrow's game," they are actually sending a positive message to themselves that they can't misinterpret. These messages carry extra weight because your children are both the sender and the recipient of the messages, and because they are the sender, they feel a greater sense of ownership of and connection to the messages, the result of which is a motivation to act on those messages.

A key goal for you is to ensure the message conduits—verbal, emotional, and behavioral, and your young athletes themselves—are aligned and communicating the same message. With this multifaceted messaging, your young athletes are "hit" with healthy messages from all directions, making it difficult for them to miss or misinterpret the messages that are sent and that you want them to receive.

Message Blockers

Have you noticed that sometimes your young athletes only need to hear a message once and they get it? And, frustratingly, that sometimes you can send a message dozens and dozens of times, and it is as if you had never sent the message at all? Welcome to the real world of sport parenting, where nothing goes as expected, what is supposed to work doesn't, what isn't assumed to work does, and what does work only works intermittently or for a limited time. It takes detective work and a real understanding of your children to figure out why some messages get through easily and others, despite your best efforts, don't seem to get through at all.

Even if you understand the messages you want to communicate to your young athletes, even if you know which conduits through which those messages are conveyed, and even if you have strategies by which to send those healthy messages, you can't be sure those messages will get through. Every time you send a message to your children, it will likely have to navigate its way through a maze of "message blockers" that can deflect, weaken, contaminate, or outright destroy your intended messages to your children in their athletic lives. If you can understand these message blockers, you can lessen their impact and increase the chances your messages will make it into the minds of your children in their athletic lives.

Unclear Messages: "Huh?"

One of the challenges of communicating messages to your young athletes is ensuring they actually understand the messages you send. The key to this understanding is conveying messages in ways that are appropriate for their level of development. I see many sports parents who send messages that seem perfectly clear to them and then can't understand why their children aren't getting those messages. Even worse, parents then blame their children for not getting their messages. The problem is that parents see their messages through their own eyes rather than those of their children. But your children don't think the way you do. You have years of experience during which you have honed your ability to interpret and understand the world (and realize how often you still miss messages). In contrast, your children are still relatively undeveloped, particularly in their athletic lives, when it comes to how they perceive, interpret, analyze, and make decisions about their world. This is why you have to walk in your children's shoes (or cleats, skates, tennis shoes, or ski boots). Ask yourself, if you were a young athlete, what message would you be getting? By doing this, you can increase the likelihood that the message your young athletes get is the very message you sent.

Disconnect Between Send and Receive: "But I Didn't Mean That."

As I mentioned earlier, the messages you send aren't always the messages your young athletes receive. This disconnect between sending and receiving can occur in several places. You may intend to send one message but end up sending another. The disconnect here is between your intention and your action. For example, you may intend to communicate to your children the message that they should pay attention to their coaches because it is the respectful thing to do and they'll also get more out of their practice time, but the actual message you send is, "I get mad at you when you're not taking your sport seriously."

The disconnect can also occur between the message you send and the message your children receive. Don't think about the message you mean to communicate, but rather the message your young athletes will likely get. Ask yourself: How clear is my message? If I were 12 years old, for instance, what message would I get? Here's an example. You work very hard at a sport that you love participating in and have a lot of success at it, demonstrated by your regular wins and medals. You want to send the message to your children that you are driven by your passion for the sport and the joy you feel from competing. But the message they get is, "My mommy competes because she loves to win." Certainly, these are two very different messages with very different implications in your young athletes' perceptions of your and their sports participation.

Infrequent Messages: "How Many Times Have I Told You?"

There are some messages your children get from you after you send them just a few times. For example, your children don't need to be told many times that it feels really good to win. But with many messages, a few times isn't enough. The frustrating reality of conveying messages about their athletic lives is that the more you "click the send button," the better the chance your young athletes will get them. So, if you don't send them a message with sufficient frequency, it may not sink in. And, let's be realistic, after a while, it gets both tiring and tedious to keep sending the messages. The result is that you give up because your children just don't get it. But giving up ensures they won't get the message and also does them a disservice because they won't gain the benefits of the message. Plus, it's easy to blame your kids because they don't pay attention, are lazy, or don't care enough about their sport. But, oftentimes, their "not getting it" is due less to them and more to your simply not sending the message enough.

The issue of message frequency is a tough one because being a parent, much less a sport parent, is difficult enough. You lead a busy life and are juggling a lot of balls every day. You have a long list of daily responsibilities that might include work, meals, housekeeping, family care, and shopping. Add in knowing your kids' practice and competition schedules, making sure they get to practices and games, and volunteering your time and energy to their sports programs and being a sport parent can be downright overwhelming. And those responsibilities don't even include taking care of yourself, for instance, getting exercise, reading a book, or spending time with your spouse or friends.

Because you're so busy, it's easy for your messages about your children's sports participation, no matter how important you know they are, to fall through the cracks. As you're dashing around with a to-do list that never seems to get done and not enough hours in the day, you might fleetingly think you'll get to those important messages. But, because family life rarely slows down, they continue to be pushed farther down on the priority list until those messages simply fall off the bottom of the list.

Sending the messages you want your young athletes to get requires several things. First, it necessitates a real commitment to those messages because they are important to their athletic lives. Second, at a very practical level, it requires just keeping those messages on your radar screen because, with so much on your plate every day, you will simply forget them. Some helpful tips include writing reminders on post-it notes and placing them where you'll see them regularly, setting reminders on your smartphone with alerts to ping or ring them back into your consciousness, and enlisting your spouse to prompt you or also sending the messages to your children.

Too Many Messages: "Do This, That, and the Other Thing."

One of the real challenges of being a young person, not even including being a young athlete, is that their "inbox" can get full fast. And, just like with e-mail, if your children can't keep up with the messages you send them, they'll either ignore or "delete" many of them. One thing you have to be careful of when you commit to conscious messaging is message overload, in other words, trying to convey too many messages to your children at one time. You may get so excited about all of the great messages you can communicate to your young athletes about their sports experience that you start hurling as many messages as possible at them at once.

Several problems arise when you become overzealous about sending messages to your children about their athletic lives. First, the messages, rather than being distinct, may amass into an incomprehensible jumble that causes them to lose their value. Second, your children may be so bombarded by messages about their sports participation—not to mention the other messages you are sending to them about their lives outside of sports—that they won't be able to focus sufficiently on any single message. The worst-case scenario is that, to avoid being overwhelmed by your messages or to try to get you to stop your messaging completely, your children tune out your messages entirely, actively resist them, or even do the exact opposite of what your messages tell them.

The best strategy is to choose and focus on a few messages that are most appropriate to your children's current level of athletic and life development. Life has a way of letting parents know what their children need to learn at any given time, and that is no less so as it relates to their sports participation. For example, if your son is getting frustrated because he isn't progressing as quickly or getting as much playing time as his best friend, you are presented with a ready-made "teachable moment" where you can send messages about patience and perseverance.

Inconsistent Messages: "You Can This Time."

Although we may not like to admit it, many of us as parents aren't as consistent as we should be. Too often, we allow our children to do some things sometimes—usually when it's expedient—but not others. For example, we make them practice their sport sometimes but let them off the hook when they don't feel like it other times. What's the message your children are getting with these inconsistent messages? At best, they don't get the messages at all. At worst, the contradictory messages confuse them so much that they choose for themselves which message works best for them, even if it isn't the one you want them to get. In the case of the aforementioned example, that means they will blow off practicing when they don't feel like it. Or even worse, they get the metamessage that being inconsistent is okay. You want to make sure you are sending your messages about their athletic lives consistently.

Conflicting Messages: "But Daddy Said . . ."

If you and your spouse send conflicting messages, you pretty much guarantee that a message won't get through to your children. These contradictory messages occur most often when parents have different values and goals about their children's sports experience. This disconnect between messages is exacerbated when there is marital conflict or a divorce that creates a contentious relationship between parents. Your young athletes will not only not get the message you want them to receive but also be confused by the contradictory messages from such credible sources and may become paralyzed with uncertainty about what your message really is and what you want them to do.

To reduce conflicting messages, parents need to look at their parenting beliefs and explore where the conflicting messages are coming from. In-depth discussions about parenting philosophies and styles, as well as values and goals related to your children's sports participation, should be prerequisites to identifying and resolving possible conflicts in the messages you send to your children. In an ideal world, you want to come to some resolution long before the messages are communicated to your children. In the real world, the sooner you can start sending harmonious messages, the better it will be for your children in their athletic lives.

Teammate Messages: "I Need to Be Accepted."

As your children get older and more of their time is spent outside your home, most notably at school and in sports, the influence of the outside world beyond your family grows. Your children's teammates are one of their most significant influences on their values, attitudes, and behavior related to their sports participation in two ways.

First, because peer acceptance is such a powerful force in the lives of young people, your children are vulnerable to the messages their teammates communicate to them directly and indirectly. Of course, this impact can be positive or negative. Teammates with healthy perspectives on sports can reinforce and support your own positive messages. Unfortunately, in turn, teammates who have unhealthy perspectives about sports can send messages that conflict with those you want your young athletes to get.

Second, as the team your children participate in begins to gel, the values, attitudes, and behaviors expressed by individual members of the team can coalesce into a team culture that envelops all of its members. What unfortunately can happen is that those teammates with the least healthy approaches to sports can also be the most vocal, in which case they play an outsized role in shaping the culture of the team. As a result, unhealthy norms get established, and it is very difficult for individual members of the team to resist those messages, however bad they are.

In either case, the most you can do is to ensure that your young athletes are participating in a youth sports program that has coaches and families that support the messages you want your children to get. Additionally, when there are teammates who communicate less positive messages, you can use them as teachable moments to discuss both healthy and unhealthy messages, explore how they impact your children, and help them to resist those messages while still staying connected to their teammates.

Coach Messages: "Do as I Say and as I Do."

The coach of your children's sports team is also a powerful source of messages for your children in their athletic lives based on the authority and respect they command, as well as the sheer amount of time they spend with your young athletes. As much as the members of the team, coaches send influential messages to their team at practices and in competitions through their words, emotions, and actions. These messages are received directly by individual team members and also have an impact on the team by shaping the team's culture.

Because of the leadership role of coaches, your young athletes will be highly receptive to their messages, healthy or not. As with the messaging from teammates, your best course of action to ensure that your children are getting positive messages from their coaches is to find youth sports programs who hire and train coaches with messages that align with your own.

Messages from the Sports Culture: "Winning Is Everything!"

Perhaps the most persuasive and insidious source of unhealthy messages to your children in their athletic lives is the youth sports culture that they are a part of, as well as the professional sports culture they are exposed to through the many forms of media. As emphasized earlier in *Raising Young Athletes*, the messaging from the youth sports culture has shifted in a truly unhealthy direction—winning is everything, early success matters, self before team—in the last few decades. Similar messages are being "broadcast" by professional and big-time college sports as well. These messages spread like a virus to youth sports administrators, coaches, and parents until they reach our young

> The sports world is an echo chamber. All it takes is one quote from a general manager and a thousand sports columns bloom.
> —Michael Lewis, American journalist[7]

athletes. The only chance your children have of resisting these unhealthy messages is for you to be aware of them, constantly send healthy messages to your children, and regularly talk to your children about both the positive and negative messages so they can make conscious choices about which messages to allow in and adopt as their own.

FIVE RULES OF MESSAGING

Given the wide and forceful sources of unhealthy messages that your children are confronted by daily in their athletic lives, you have to marshal every tool and trick at your disposal to ensure your messages get through to them and the harmful ones are held at bay. There are five rules to help ensure your messages get through to your children loud and clear. You should use multiple conduits, use loudspeaker and stealth messages, let your children help shape your messages, be simple and clear, and be active.

Use Multiple Conduits

As I'm sure you realize, children receive, process, and learn information in different ways. They can take in messages visually (by watching), auditorily (by hearing), or tactilely (by feeling), and by reading or writing. You can judge how your children best receive messages and then send your messages through the conduits that play to your children's information-processing strengths, increasing the likelihood your messages will get through.

At the same time, I recommend that you send messages through multiple conduits, including their dominant and nondominant modes. In doing so, you are communicating your messages to them through multiple and diverse pathways that are processed through different psychological and neurological systems. The result is that your messages have a better chance of getting through and being ingrained more deeply and completely.

So, when you want to send a message to your young athletes, consider the different ways in which you can communicate the message to them. For example, let's say you want to convey the message that they should focus on having fun in their sport and not take it too seriously. To best transmit this message, you can do the following:

- Talk to them about the benefits of keeping sports fun and light.
- Model your message by having fun at their games.
- Make choices indicating that their sports aren't that important (e.g., don't attend every game, let your children take days off if they need a break).
- Keep your own sports participation fun and light.
- Show examples of athletes and parents in the media who take their sports too seriously.

Use Loudspeaker and Stealth Messages

You can convey messages to your children about their sports experiences either directly or indirectly. "Loudspeaker" messages include telling them the message you want them to get, pointing it out in other people, or referring to media stories that illustrate the specific message. These straightforward messages ensure that there is no confusion about their intent and that your young athletes are paying attention and focused on the message. For instance, during dinner, you might talk to them about how they might respond emotionally to a difficult loss. The risks with direct messages are that your children may get tired of your attempts at obvious messaging and tune out your messages (as they get older, your messages may still be good, but they don't want you to be the messenger.)

In contrast, "stealth" messages are those in which your young athletes are completely unaware that you are sending them messages. Returning to the example in the previous paragraph, after a tough loss that they are upset about, you are calm, empathetic, and ask them where they want to have lunch. In this stealth message, you communicate to them that you are there to support them, but the loss isn't that big a deal. They don't notice the message they are getting from you, but it is, nonetheless, a powerful one that will sneak past them and into their minds.

Let Your Children Help Shape Your Messages

Your young athletes have an amazing ability to let you know about the messages they might need at any given time. It's up to you to have your "radio tuned to their frequency" so you pick up on those messages. Your children will frequently have experiences, challenges, and reactions in their athletic lives that signal an opportunity to communicate a healthy message to them. For example, after scoring the winning goal, your daughter engages in what you consider to be excessive celebration. Her behavior may be an alert to send some messages about the value of humility.

Your children can also let you know the way in which they will be most receptive to a message, helping you choose a conduit that has the best chance of being heard and accepted. For instance, if they are frustrated and angry with how they played in a game, they will probably not be in a state of mind in which they will be open to having a discussion about their feelings. In this case, instead of trying to talk to them directly about their feelings, the best way to send them a message is to just express a different and counterbalancing set of emotions by giving them a hug and kiss, and telling them that you love them.

Be Simple and Clear

You have to remember that your children don't think as you do. Whether your young athletes get the messages you send them depends on their level of development. As a result, tailor your messages to fit their current maturity. Young children, because their cognitive, emotional, and language capabilities are not yet fully developed, need messages to be simple and unambiguous. And as your children develop, you can increase the complexity of your messages. At the same time, I believe in the KISS principle. No, not "Keep It Simple, Stupid," as it is often known, but rather, "Keep It Simple, Smart." So even with children who are more mature, there is nothing like a simple and straightforward message that you know will get through.

As I discuss earlier in this chapter, the messages you intend to send may not always be the ones they receive. Because of this disconnect, make sure your words, emotions, and actions unambiguously communicate the message you want to convey. Before you send your young athletes a message, step into their shoes and consider what your message might look like to them. Ask yourself whether your means of conveying the message is the best way for them to get it. After you've sent the message, see if they seem to have gotten it. If they have, pat yourself on the back. If not, figure out where you went wrong and recalibrate your message until they finally do get it.

Be Active

Sending positive messages to your children about their athletic lives through your words can be a useful way to educate them about healthy values, attitudes, and behavior. But talk can be confusing, especially if what you say conflicts with what you do. A powerful way to convey positive messages to your children is through actions, both yours and theirs. If you want your children to really get the messages you communicate to them, behave in accordance with those messages. And, even more powerfully, if you can get your children to act in ways that are consistent with your messages, you know you've got them.

Sending healthy messages to your young athletes is also not a part-time job, "I'll do it when I feel like it" sort of thing. The reality is that your children are being bombarded by messages from other sources in their sports world that are truly unhealthy. You can't just play defense because your messages will be overwhelmed and lost in the onslaught. You must go on the offensive and do some bombarding of your own, but with positive messages, of course. The best way to counter the harmful messages from the youth sports culture is to surround your children with a world of beneficial messages. The more conduits through which you can send messages to your children, the greater the likelihood they will either not see or just plain ignore the detrimental messages and get the life-affirming messages about sports you want them to.

FOUR MESSAGES I WANT YOU TO GET

To conclude this chapter, there are four messages I want you to get from our discussion of messaging your young athletes. First, as I note at the beginning of the chapter, my central theme is that *your children become the messages they get the most.* This perspective means your young athletes will develop the values, attitudes, and behaviors about their sports experiences based on the messages that are most frequent and most compelling to them. As a result, you want to ensure that they are receiving predominantly positive messages from you and your spouse, your family, their immediate sports world (e.g., teammates, coaches, program), and the sports culture they are surrounded by.

Second, the challenge for you is that, from teammates to coaches to teams to the youth sports culture to the prevailing culture of sports in general, your children may be getting more unhealthy than healthy messages. This harmful imbalance in messaging means you need to do everything you can to *take control of your young athletes' messages*. Your only chance to counteract that onslaught of outside messages is to actively create a steady stream of your own positive messages, through your words, emotions, actions, activities, and the healthy messages of other people and institutions that align with your own, which can counterbalance and counteract the many harmful messages they are certain to receive in their athletic lives.

Third, to accomplish the first two items, you must *know what messages you want to send and send the messages you want*. As related earlier in the chapter, you can't play defense when it comes to messaging. You can't just hope your young athletes receive positive messages in their athletic lives. Rather, you need to deliberately identify the messages you believe are most relevant for your children in their current sports participation and proactively send them using the aforementioned strategies. This consciousness in your messaging also has to be ongoing. Because your young athletes' sports experiences change and new unhealthy messages come to the fore, you must adapt to the changing athletic landscape by creating messages that respond in kind.

Finally, you must practice what I call the 3 Ps + 1R. You must be *patient* in your messaging, because it can take days, weeks, months, and even years for your young athletes to get and ingrain the messages you send them. You need to be *persistent* because it's easy to get frustrated and want to give up when you don't see immediate results from your messaging efforts. You have to *persevere* in the face of bad messages from the outside world and your children not getting your messages, resisting your messages, and adopting opposing messages. And, for the sake of your children, you must be absolutely *relentless* in your healthy messaging and your vigilance in rebuffing unhealthy messages. You must simply decide that, no matter what the outside sports world throws at your young athletes, you will never, ever ease up or back down, because to give up on your messaging would be akin to giving up on your children in their athletic lives, and as a sport parent who loves your young athletes, that just wouldn't do.

> It's the repetition of affirmations that leads to belief. And once that belief becomes a deep conviction, things begin to happen.
> —Muhammad Ali, legendary boxing champion[8]

DOS AND DON'TS
FOR SPORT PARENTS

Being a sport parent is no small feat, and it's certainly a much bigger job than just being a parent. Above and beyond the basics of parenting, including clothing, feeding, loving, supporting (materially and emotionally), and educating your children, as a sport parent, you must also pay for your children's sport, ensure they have the proper gear, get them to practices and competitions, volunteer your time, and don't forget to help them through the emotional roller coaster that is youth sports. And those responsibilities don't even take into account the toll being a sport parent takes on you, financially, emotionally, its impact on your marriage, the opportunity costs you and your family incur, and in terms of your own needs and interests. In *Raising Young Athletes*, I've attempted to help you navigate this rough, yet hopefully rewarding, terrain to the benefit of your young athletes, yourself, and your family writ large. Ultimately, my goal in sharing *Raising Young Athletes* with you is to provide you with the insights, information, and tools you need to raise not only great athletes but also great people and make their sports experiences a positive and affirming experience for your entire family.

In the first two chapters of *Raising Young Athletes*, I focus on how you can help your children lay a solid foundation for their enjoyment of and success in sports by instilling healthy attitudes that will propel them toward their athletic goals and remove unhealthy attitudes that obstruct their path to those goals. In chapter 3, I explore the different roles and responsibilities you can assume in their athletic lives and how to take on the roles that will best support your young athletes and avoid responsibilities that might interfere with their sports experiences. Chapter 4 is even more practical, describing the importance of the messages your children get from the many levels of the sports world and how you can ensure they get healthy messages that foster their athletic and personal development. In sum, I've given you a tremendous amount of information to help you be the best sport parent you can be.

DOS FOR SPORT PARENTS

But, if you're like most sport parents I know (or like me, for that matter), all that deep stuff is really interesting and valuable, but what you really want are clear guidelines of what you should and shouldn't do with your young athletes and the sports world they inhabit. To that end, chapter 5 is devoted to precisely that. I describe what I believe you should do and should not do with

> Kids play with joy in their heart. Parents and coaches: Please don't rob them of that. — *MOTA (Mind of the Athlete forum)*[1]

yourself, other parents, coaches, and your children to be the best sport parent you can be while also surviving the sports season without driving yourself and your children crazy.

Do for Yourself

I'm a big believer that you can't do what's best for your young athletes before you do what's best for you in your children's athletic lives. This may sound selfish, but I also believe that an unhappy sport parent can't possibly be a positive force in their children's lives. To that end, here are my recommendations for what you should do for yourself as you share your children's sports journey with them.

Embrace the Good Times

When you join your children on the emotional roller coaster of youth sports, you really don't know what you're signing up for until it's too late to get off. Until you're living it, no one can adequately describe what the experience is like. It is, as you quickly learn, not all fun and games; in fact, it is often neither fun nor games.

Yet, like your children, if you only focus on the downs, their sports experiences won't be enjoyable for you or them. That's why it's so important to truly embrace and highlight the good times. As you either have seen or will see, the moments your young athletes have are truly special; learning a new skill, finding new and lasting friends, overcoming a struggle, and, yes, experiencing the victories are moments to savor with your young athletes. So, when those moments arise, recognize and acknowledge them in your own mind, and also highlight and share them with your children because those moments help gird you for the challenges that are also part and parcel of all sports experiences. Moreover, when you embrace those good times and sear them into your brain, they, in time, turn into memories that can last a lifetime.

Get Vicarious Pleasure

Being a sport parent isn't easy, to be sure. Yet, one of the great rewards of doing what we do in our children's athletic lives involves getting vicarious pleasure from their sports participation. Let's be realistic. When we sign our kids up for sports, we are investing ourselves in that athletic involvement. As I've talked about, too much investment on your part is unhealthy. Yet, too little investment isn't healthy either. The vicarious pleasure you experience when your young athletes "win" is part of your reward for that investment. I put "win" in quotes because wins can mean much more than just victories, whether holding their own against a better player, continuing to give a great effort when far behind, or persevering in difficult weather conditions. The pride you feel in those efforts is palatable, healthy, and powerful payback for all you do for your children as they pursue their sports goals. So, rather than being a guilty pleasure, allow yourself to fully experience your kids' athletic lives vicariously.

Enjoy Yourself at Competitions

As I discuss in chapter 4, you send messages to your young athletes when they are competing. One of the most important messages you can send to them is that you are enjoying yourself. If they see you having fun, your children are more likely to have fun themselves. Enjoying yourself at competitions isn't always easy because there are a lot of reasons not to. For example, for outdoor sports, the weather can be miserable, whether brutally hot, horribly cold, or raining or snowing. In many sports, there is a lot of sitting and standing around waiting for competitions to begin. And as your young athletes move up the competitive ladder and join traveling teams it means time away from home; frequently separating from your spouse and other children; and often going to less-than-glamorous destinations for games, tournaments, and meets.

So, you should actively look for ways to enjoy yourself aside from watching your children compete. The following are some suggestions:

- Nurture friendships with other sport parents and enjoy socializing with them between and during competitions.
- Visit interesting places near where competitions are being held.
- Find time for yourself, for example, take a walk, read, or get some exercise.
- Use downtime to connect with family and friends you are away from.
- Learn more about the sport in which your children are participating by keeping statistics or focusing on a particular aspect of the sport.
- Volunteer at competitions.

Get a Life

In chapter 2, I share my thoughts on becoming overly invested in your children's athletic lives to the point where it becomes the dominant source of meaning and satisfaction in your own life. If how your young athletes perform in competitions substantially dictates how you feel about yourself, you will certainly make yourself and them miserable on game day by being stressed, worried, and unhappy.

A gift you can give yourself and your children in their sport is to make sure you have a life of your own that is enjoyable, fulfilling, and meaningful, whether your career or an avocation. In doing so, you unburden your children from having to provide that satisfaction and validation for you. Taking this approach to your young athletes when they compete means you are unburdened from the excessive weight of overinvestment and free to appreciate your children's involvement, enjoy their efforts and accomplishments, and share their athletic experience with them for their own sake.

> In the past, you'd have groups of kids . . . playing unorganized sports for fun. Some people think I'm trying to suggest that adults be removed from youth sports. I'm not. I'm suggesting the adult ego be removed from youth sports. —Bob Bigelow, former NBA player[2]

Do with Other Parents

When you sign your children up for a sport, they're not the only ones making a commitment. Instead, you're also signing yourself up for a commitment of time, energy, and money. In doing so, you are joining a club of its own comprised of other sport parents. Aside from school, your children's athletic lives can become the focal point of your family's lives and a nexus of your own social world.

Make Friends

You will be around these same sport parents, at a minimum, for a season and, at a maximum, for as long as a decade or more if your children make a long-term commitment to a sport. Because of the ongoing presence of much the same group of parents for an extended period of time, I encourage you to actively build friendships with other sport parents. When you build a strong network of like-minded sport parents, you will have more fun, feel more deeply connected to your children's sports participation, feel supported during difficult times, revel together in the high times, commiserate collectively during times of struggle, and share practical responsibilities like driving to practices and competitions.

Volunteer

As I note earlier in *Raising Young Athletes*, youth sports are driven by parent volunteers who fill so many vital roles that enable the various sports to function, including coaches, managers, fundraisers, event organizers, officials, referees and umpires, timers, and the list goes on. When you team up with other sport parents to volunteer for the many roles and responsibilities that exist in youth sports programs, it serves several purposes that benefit your children.

You become more connected to their sport, which sends a message that you care enough about their involvement to devote your precious time and energy to their athletic lives. You enjoy yourself more. You learn more about

> Volunteers do not necessarily have the time; they have the heart.
> —*Elizabeth Andrews, Welsh political activist*[3]

their sport and, in doing so, can make better decisions about the path your young athletes might follow in the sport. Lastly, you send the message to your young athletes that, although the sport is theirs, you are fully there to support their participation, efforts, and dreams.

Police Your Own Ranks

Having been around youth sports all of my life, as a young athlete, a sport psychologist, and a parent, I can attest to the fact that the vast majority of sport parents are well intentioned and typically do what is best for their children. At the same time, there is always a minority of parents, unfortunately quite vocal, who can step outside of what is considered appropriate and healthy by most sport parents and act in ways that are misplaced and harmful to young athletes. I believe that it is up to the parent community of your children's sports to play an active role in policing their own ranks, both in preventing and reacting to objectionable behavior on the part of parents, for example, insulting officials, yelling at their children, or fighting with other parents.

The first step in policing your own ranks is to provide clarity to the parents in your children's athletic community about what is acceptable and unacceptable behavior. An effective orientation as parents enter a youth sports organization and ongoing opportunities for parent education are both helpful tools for detailing what is considered appropriate and inappropriate conduct in youth sports settings. Practical guidelines like those offered in chapter 5 and the development of a sport parent code of conduct that parents must sign make clear how parents are expected to act and what is not allowed at practices and competitions.

These preventive measures can also be useful when sport parents transgress. Rather than these parents being able to plead ignorance in defense of their behavior, a public code of conduct and clearly stated guidelines can be referred back to as reminders of what they signed up for and what will and will not be tolerated. Such materials can be developed and disseminated with a particular youth sports program, established with a local league, or offered by such organizing associations as an Olympic national governing body. Moreover, when a tight-knit community of parents has been created within a team, a healthy culture of sport parenting can exert "pressure" on its members to act within the accepted norms of behavior. Additionally, this connection and cohesiveness enables willing parents to gently confront the offending parents and remind them of the code of conduct, the harm their behavior can cause, and what the parent community expects of its members.

If this parent-to-parent enforcement isn't effective, parents have the right to report the inappropriate behavior to the youth sport program's administrators. They may have the authority to threaten sanctions as a means of curbing the unacceptable behavior and en-

> Reminders from your child: I'm a kid; it's a game; my coach is a volunteer; the officials are human; no college scholarships will be handed out today. —*Pleasanton, California, Little League sign*[4]

couraging adherence to the agreed-upon norms of suitable behavior. Sanctions might include being banned from competitions or, in a worst-case scenario, kicking the child off of the team for the bad behavior of their parents.

Do with Coaches

The coaches of your young athletes have a huge impact on them in so many ways, both related and unrelated to their sports participation. Coaches affect your children physically, psychologically, emotionally, and socially. Given the breadth of this influence, you want to make sure they are your allies in helping your children achieve their athletic goals. If any conflict, discomfort, or tension exists between you and their coaches, your young athletes will certainly sense it, and it will interfere with their enjoyment, performance, and progress in their sport. When you and their coaches stand shoulder to shoulder in support of your young athletes, your children will likely experience enjoyment and success in their sport and the game of life.

Be Allies with the Coaches

The parent–coach relationship is a vital, yet sometimes tenuous, connection to children's athletic lives. The degree to which parents and coaches can collaborate and communicate, with the best interests of the young athletes in mind, can often determine the experiences the children have in their chosen sport. You want to do everything you can to align your own needs and goals for your children with those of their coaches, with the intention of making sure both of your efforts work in harmony to maximize your young athletes' enjoyment and development in their sport.

> Our coach leads by example, is dedicated and determined, teaches teamwork, motivates and listens, builds character, challenges and develops, is committed to our team, is our biggest fan. —*Anonymous*[5]

Your children's coaches also work hard for them, and especially at the lower levels of sports, they either volunteer their time or receive little pay for their commitment of time and energy. As such, they deserve your respect, kindness, support, and appreciation. And, if they view you as their ally, they are more likely to ally themselves with you, to the benefit of your children. You can facilitate a strong relationship between yourself and your children's coaches by sharing with them your goals for your children's sports participation and listening to their own goals for your children. If you and they are philosophically aligned, you provide your young athletes with a solid foundation from which they can pursue their sports goals.

Leave the Coaching to the Coaches

When your children immerse themselves in a sport, you naturally want to help them develop as much and as quickly as you can. In this age of "everyone can be an expert" by reading articles online and watching videos on YouTube, it's easy to persuade yourself that you know enough about a sport to provide good coaching to your young athletes. But, unless you have actual competitive or coaching experience in a sport, you're really just fooling yourself. In doing so, you are actually interfering with, rather than facilitating, your children's athletic development for several reasons.

First, you will probably give them bad instruction or feedback that isn't appropriate for their level of development. Second, correct or not, your feedback will muddy the waters of the instruction their coaches are giving them, rendering it confusing at best and ineffective at worst. Third, you undermine your children's confidence in your coaches because you're sending them the message that you don't trust them to do their job.

So, please leave the coaching to the coaches. Remember that they are experts, they know what they're doing, and, at a practical level, you're paying them to coach your children, so let them.

Support Your Children's Coaches

Coaching isn't an easy job. Coaches have a lot on their plates, including planning practices, scheduling competitions, organizing travel, getting equipment, raising money, collaborating with the rest of the coaching staff, and, yes, dealing with parents. Oh, and they also have to actually coach your children. Given the commitment that your family is making to your children's sport and how busy their coaches are, you should give them any support they need so they can do the best job they can.

I encourage you to look for all of the ways you can support your children's coaches and then, either just you or in collaboration with other parents, unburden them of as much as you can so you can free them to do what they are fundamentally there to do, namely, develop young athletes and people. Some of the responsibilities you could assume might include scheduling travel, bringing drinks and snacks to practices, loading and unloading equipment, packing a lunch for them, the list goes on. Here's a simple calculus: More free time and fewer responsibilities for your coaches equals more time and energy devoted to coaching your children.

Communicate with Your Children's Coaches

One of the greatest gifts you can give your children in their athletic lives is positive and healthy relationships with their coaches in which there are open lines of communication in both directions. Effective communication is beneficial to your young athletes in two ways.

First, your children's coaches get to know and see them in ways that you don't. Your children likely behave, interact, and perform in sports differently than they might with your family or at school. When they share their observations about your kids with you, you see them through an entirely different set of lenses, which can enrich your own view of them and help you to better understand who they are and, in doing so, respond to their needs and goals. For example, on the affirming side, you may hear about a child who is far more confident and resilient than you have come to know at home or school. Conversely, on the disappointing side, you may also hear about a child who is less attentive and respectful than you have come to know. In either case, you can use this information to paint a more realistic portrait of your children with the benefit that you are better able to meet them where they are rather than where you think they are or wish them to be.

Second, your children's coaches only see them in a narrow setting, namely, at practice and in competitions. As such, they may develop an impression of your young athletes that is based on limited information, which might also result in a less-than-accurate representation of who your children are. You can help both their coaches and, by extension, your children by helping their coaches develop a broader, deeper, and more nuanced view of them. You can also keep their coaches informed and up-to-date on relevant issues happening outside of your kids' athletic lives. For instance, their coaches may, at one practice, see an athlete who is unusually frustrated and angry, but if you've let them know there is considerable conflict at home or they're having challenges at school, the coaches can act appropriately with empathy, support, and encouragement.

Do for Your Children

What you do with, for, and to your children matters a lot. Although you can certainly influence your children by what you do with yourself, other parents, and their coaches, the most impact you can have comes from your direct interaction with them. To that end, here are some recommendations on what you can do for your children that will help them to enjoy their sport the most, find the most success, and get the most out of their athletic experiences.

Provide Guidance, but Don't Dictate

Particularly early in their athletic lives, your children don't know much about their sport or what it takes to be an athlete. So, they will look to you for guidance in all aspects of their sports experiences, whether related to what level to compete at, which club to join, what equipment they need, how much to practice, and how important their sport should be to them. Certainly, as they immerse themselves in a sport, they will become more informed and better equipped to make their own decisions, but there will always be a time and place in which your input will be needed and appreciated.

From when your young athletes pick up a sport, you will need to micromanage them because they simply lack the wherewithal to know what's best for them. In many cases, you will be making the decisions for them. The danger is when that micromanagement becomes a habit that persists as your children get older and are capable of more fully owning their sport and making their own decisions. During this transition as your children mature and become experienced athletes, you also want to transition from micromanagement to management in which you strike a balance between taking care of aspects of their sport that aren't their responsibility (e.g., paying for club fees and driving to practices until they have their driver's license), while ceding responsibility for those parts of their sport they are capable of managing (e.g., planning their practice schedule, coordinating with their coach, selecting their equipment, and packing their gear bags).

Emphasize Fun and Other Benefits

As detailed in chapter 4, your young athletes will be getting many messages from teammates, coaches, club administrators, and the larger youth sports culture that it's all about results. Sadly, those messages will not always support your children's sports efforts. You need to counter those messages by emphasizing and prioritizing for your young athletes the many benefits of sports participation. Fun, healthy competition, and the development of essential life skills are just a few of the many wonderful advantages your children can gain from sports. The chances are infinitesimally small that your children will become athletic superstars (or even compete in college), but sports can still be a wonderful and impactful life experience that can positively shape their futures.

Show Interest

One of the most affirming and confidence-building things you can do for your children is simply show interest in their athletic lives. When you indicate that you care about their sports participation, they feel valued and supported, and know that you will be there for them through the ups and downs.

You can show your interest in many ways. A basic, yet powerful, way is to ask them questions about their sports experiences, for example, what they are working on in practice, what they're enjoying about it and what they're not, how they feel about competitions, ways they are improving, and areas they are working on in their sport.

Another obvious way to show interest is simply to be present and involved in your children's athletic lives. You can do this by shopping with them for their sports gear, helping them practice at home if they ask, driving them to practice, and attending competitions. The simple act of being there sends a powerful message that you care about their sports involvement.

Encourage Other Interests

There is a lot of pressure these days for young athletes to specialize in a sport early and commit entirely to the sport to the exclusion of other activities. The message that sport parents are getting is that if their children aren't on the specialization train earlier, they're going to be left behind at the station for good. Yet, as I note earlier in *Raising Young Athletes*, expert opinion and scientific research suggest that this "full steam ahead" approach to youth sports development not only doesn't work in terms of accelerating athletic development but also hurts children physically and psychologically.

There is no doubt that specialization at some point is necessary if young athletes have big aspirations in their sport. At the same time, the professional consensus is that having other interests outside of sport and balance in their lives offers some key benefits, including increased motivation, lower rates of burnout, fewer injuries, and better long-term prospects in the sport. To that end, I encourage you to support your children in finding and maintaining involvement in activities beyond sport, including specific school subjects, the performing arts, and charitable work.

Provide a Healthy Perspective

Like so many aspects of their athletic lives, your children may be getting truly unhealthy messages from their teammates, coaches, and the wider youth sports culture about success and failure ("It's all about winning!"), and they may very well come to define success and failure in those harmful terms. You can prevent this from happening by adopting and conveying healthier messages to them about success and failure. If you do, your young athletes will likely come to define success and failure in the ways you do and ways that will not only encourage their athletic efforts but also foster their positive personal development.

I encourage you to get clear on your own personal definitions of success and failure, and ensure they are healthy. As I discussed earlier, success should primarily be about your children giving their best effort, having fun, being good teammates, and gaining the benefits of sports participation. Success as defined as winning should only be the result of that definition and icing on the cake from your children's

> Along this path pass the greatest baseball players you will ever know—your children. Be with them, encourage them, help them be as good as they can be, but most of all at the end of the day, win or lose, tell them you love them, for they are the most precious gift. —*San Jose Athletic Association sign*[6]

efforts. Failure, in turn, is the absence of that definition of success. Although you cannot completely protect your young athletes from the toxic messages related to success and failure, providing a healthier perspective will diminish that impact and give them a more positive way of looking at success and failure.

Be Positive and Calm

As mentioned previously, youth sports can feel like a roller coaster for children and parents alike. Big jumps in performance, runaway victories, and come-from-behind wins, as well as slow progress, setbacks, and devastating losses, are par for the course for your young athletes. That roller coaster ride can also be very emotional, ranging from excitement, joy, pride, and inspiration to anxiety, frustration, disappointment, and despair.

These challenges that your children face every day in their sports participation can be both uplifting and discouraging. You can help ensure that their athletic experiences are positive and beneficial by providing two things to your young athletes. First, offer them regular encouragement that will bolster their confidence when things are going well and gird their confidence when it has taken a hit. Win, lose, or epic fail, a hug, a kiss, a "Keep at it," a "I believe in you," or your own personal version of encouragement goes a long way in helping your children weather the rough seas of their sports involvement.

Second, that emotional roller coaster can be really tough on young athletes when their results go south. If your own emotions go in that direction as well, you are adding insult to injury; they are upset, and they will be able to see that their results have caused you to be upset too. No matter how your children perform, you want to project—and hopefully actually feel—an air of calm and cool empathy. Your composed presence during an emotional storm sends a powerfully positive message to your children in their athletic lives that, although you recognize it is an upsetting moment for them, for you, it's just part of sports, you have it in perspective, you are there entirely for them, and they will be alright.

Emphasize Process over Results

As I discuss earlier in this book, one of the greatest gifts you can give your young athletes is to emphasize process over results. Quite simply, you should never talk about results with your children. When they bring up results, immediately redirect them to what enabled them to get those results. This focus is so beneficial because your children can control the process, that is, what they need to do to perform their best, but not their results (only, to some extent, by controlling the process).

When your children direct their attention to the process, they gain several important benefits. First, they don't feel the weight of expectations and pressure that comes from a focus on results. Second, they are more calm and relaxed as they approach a competition. Finally, they feel more confident and comfortable when they compete. The paradoxical end result when your children focus on the process is that they are more likely to perform well and get the results they want.

Intervene in Bad Behavior

Whether your children experience success or failure in their athletic lives, that does not give them license to behave in unacceptable ways at practices or competitions. Inappropriate behavior can include excessive celebration, teasing or bullying teammates or opponents, having a tantrum after a loss, cheating, or being a bad sport. If you see or learn about such behavior in their sports participation, you must intervene immediately and appropriately. By ignoring it, you send a message of implicit approval. You can communicate your values and priorities concerning their athletic lives by discussing acceptable and unacceptable behavior in their sports involvement, setting clear expectations, and enforcing consequences when your children violate agreed-upon norms of appropriate behavior.

Let Your Kids Take a Break When Needed

Your young athletes have only so much fuel in their gas tanks. When your children combine the time and energy associated with their school responsibilities with a commitment to the time, physical, and mental demands of sports, they can come to feel stressed, exhausted, and overwhelmed, and their gas tank can run low. This burden usually results in a decline in enjoyment, motivation, effort, and performance. In extreme cases, young athletes may even say they want to quit their sport altogether.

If your children experience this reaction, it's easy to think they're just being lazy or ungrateful for the time and effort you devote to their athletic lives. But that response on your part only adds to the weight they feel on their shoulders and exacerbates the problem. Instead, I encourage you to recognize how busy and stressful your children's lives can be and, rather than actually wanting to quit their sport, that they may simply need an occasional break to rest, recover, and recharge their batteries. A short time away often reminds them of how much they love their sport and helps them get their "mojo" back, so they return with renewed commitment and energy.

Give Your Children Space

One of the most beneficial aspects of your children's sports participation involves the challenges it presents requiring them to figure out how they want to respond. Particularly when your young athletes are struggling, they often need time and space to just mull over the situation and decide how best to proceed. These situations may include a disappointing competitive result, a performance slump, a disagreement with a teammate, or a conflict with a coach.

In these circumstances, you may feel compelled to step in and attempt to resolve the problem for your children. This immediate reaction on your part, although well intended, would do your young athletes a disservice. When these situations arise, rather than jumping right in to either comfort them or solve the issue, I encourage you to give them the time and space to figure it out on their own. If they do, you've given them a wonderful gift of emotional management, problem solving, decision making, and conflict resolution that will last a lifetime. If they aren't able to completely solve the problem themselves, they will come to you for your support and guidance on their own terms when they are ready.

Keep a Sense of Humor

As I suggest in *Raising Young Athletes*, you and your young athletes can take sports pretty darned seriously. The problem is that such an intense view of youth sports both interferes with successful performance and sucks the enjoyment out of children's athletic experiences. As a result, keeping a sense of humor during the inevitable highs and lows of sports participation is another wonderful gift you can give your children. When it is so easy for your young athletes to go to the "dark side" when they struggle in their sport, your smiles, having fun, and your light demeanor offer an important message and a powerful counterbalance to those dark forces that can drag your children down. When your view of your children's sports participation is light and playful, those feelings will be contagious. If you're having fun at your kids' sports events, they're more likely to keep their involvement in perspective and have fun too.

> Parenting without a sense of humor is like being an accountant who sucks at math. —*Anonymous*[7]

Give Your Kids Unconditional Love

Conditional love is the most harmful message you can communicate to your children in their athletic lives. When you express your love—through attention, affection, and gifts—when your young athletes are successful, and withdraw your love—through emotional distance or anger—when they fail, you are doing potentially permanent harm to them as athletes and, far more importantly, as people. If your children come to believe that every time they compete, your love for them is on the line, you are creating a situation that can only result in bad emotions, bad experiences, bad results, and bad feelings toward you.

If you get only one thing from *Raising Young Athletes*, make sure it is that you must express your love to your children unconditionally in every aspect of their athletic lives, whether before, during, or after competitions. This potent message tells your kids that your love for them will be strong and constant regardless of how they do in their sports participation. This recognition alone removes so many of the obstacles discussed in chapter 2 and frees the young athletes to pursue their goals with commitment, confidence, and gusto.

DON'TS FOR SPORT PARENTS

As a general rule, I much prefer to focus on the positives of behavior, so I always emphasize what parents can *do* to help their young athletes achieve their goals and have great experiences in their sport. At the same time, the reality is that many parents don't always do the right thing for their children (despite the best of intentions). In these cases, I've found it helpful to also describe what I consider to be the wrong things to do because it creates awareness and acts as a boundary of what is healthy and unhealthy behavior for sport parents. The following is what I believe you *don't* want to do with yourself, other parents, coaches, and especially your young athletes.

Don't for Yourself

At the heart of "Don't for Yourself" is your ability to keep your children's athletic lives at a reasonable distance from your own. Of course, you want to keep their sports participation close enough to care deeply about that involvement, while keeping yourself far enough away so that your focus is always on their interests, needs, and goals rather than your own.

Base Your Self-Esteem on Your Children's Athletic Lives

A key theme throughout *Raising Young Athletes* is the danger of becoming overly invested in your children's athletic lives to the point where you base your self-esteem on how they perform and the results they produce in their sport. If you place the weight of your self-worth on your children's shoulders, you are putting a crushing weight on them that will pretty much guarantee either failure or profound unhappiness (or both). Additionally, you'll also be profoundly unhappy because your children failed to make you feel good about yourself (not their job, of course). If you don't have other parts of your life (e.g., marriage, career, avocations) that give you good feelings and ego gratification, I have three words for you: GET A LIFE!

Care Too Much about Results

As I've stressed before, the chances of your young athletes "making it" in sports, meaning, at a minimum, competing in college and, at a maximum, reaching the pros or the Olympics, are a near-statistical impossibility. So, you shouldn't care too much about how your children do in their sport. If you do, you'll only make yourself and your children miserable. Instead, you should care about the physical, psychological, emotional, and social benefits I describe in *Raising Young Athletes* that they will receive from their commitment to a sport.

Lose Perspective

With the attention, money, and fame that awaits the few lucky children who reach the highest level of sport, it's easy to lose perspective on its importance in the "food chain" of life. Sure, sports may be really important to your children, and it's that priority in their lives that enables them to commit to and get the most out of it. But, as the parent, you should see it otherwise.

One reality that should be obvious to all sport parents but often isn't is that sports are pretty darned unimportant in the grand scheme of things. Certainly, no matter how involved you are in your children's athletic lives, if you step back a bit, you'll be able to put it in perspective relative to everything else that is going on in your family's lives and in the world at large. That's not to say that there isn't value in youth sports. To the contrary, as I convey throughout *Raising Young Athletes*, sports are wonderful for their fun, physical benefits, and ability to teach essential life skills. But if you lose sight of what's really important in your and their lives, your children won't get any of the benefits and suffer many costs.

> Keep calm. It's just a game.
> —*Anonymous*[8]

Don't with Other Parents

Make Enemies of Other Parents

If your children stay involved in sports for years to come, you'll be seeing the same parents every weekend for the next decade or more. One of the most unpleasant experiences sport parents can have is being forced to see and be around other parents on a regular basis with whom there have been conflicts or ill feelings. It is really awkward and uncomfortable, and sucks the enjoyment out of what should be a great time supporting your young athletes. Of course, you'll come across some parents who aren't your cup of tea, and there are going to be ill feelings and conflicts along the way as kids and teams vie for starting position, wins, standings, and advancement. But it's just not fun being forced to be around people with whom you don't get along. Plus, your children will feel the vibe, and it will detract from their enjoyment. My motto with other parents is, "Be kind, be accepting, be grown up!"

Talk about Other Parents

As with any community, there are going to be parents who are members of a team's "in" group and those who aren't. And this divergence can cause gossip to run rampant. There are always going to be parents who are different or simply do things with which you don't agree. But talking *about* other parents is petty and unproductive. Instead, I recommend that you talk *with* them, not about them. If parents you know are different (they probably know they are) and don't seem to fit in, instead of gossiping about and marginalizing them, why not bring them into the fold. If you have problems with some parents, why not talk with them about it? You may find there is more common ground than you think. And it sure beats wasting all that negative energy talking about and avoiding them.

Don't with Coaches

Interfere with Coaches' Coaching

You pay the children's coaches good money (probably not enough) to help them achieve their sports goals. Why would you want to get in the way of your children's coaches doing their job? You can interfere with their coaching in several ways. First, you can try to coach your own kids. This practice is usually a bad idea because, unless you played or coached the sport at a high level, you probably don't know what you're talking about. Also, when you coach your kids, you wear hats that can be confusing to them—your parent hat and your coach hat. When you're coaching them, they don't necessarily know which hat you're wearing. Second, your attempts at coaching get in the way of their coaches' coaching. For example, you might tell your young athletes to do one thing technically when their coaches are telling them to do something completely different. Of course, you have a right to give input and receive feedback about your children, but it should never step on the toes of the coaches' efforts or occur during practices or at competitions when you want the coaches focused on your children.

Work at Cross-Purposes

There are few things more harmful to your children's sports experiences than you having a conflict with their coaches. Whether the difference is philosophical (e.g., values, priorities, goals) or practical (e.g., equipment, training volume, competitive schedule), your children will be the ones who suffer for it. You want to ensure that you and their coaches are aligned in the whys, hows, whats, wheres, and whens of their athletic lives. If there is a conflict, you have four choices. You can accept the coaches' perspective. You can find common ground and ignore the differences. You and the coaches can compromise on the points of disagreement. Or you can find another coach or youth sports program that better fits your needs and goals for your children.

Don't for Your Children

Show Negative Emotions When Attending a Competition

Your children are highly attuned to your emotions and use that information to determine how they should think, feel, and behave. If you're stressed out before a competition, they will probably get anxious too. If you express frustration and anger during a competition, they will see that you're not happy with how they are performing. If you are noticeably disappointed after a competition, they will likely feel that they are letting you down. No matter how much you try to cover up your feelings and attempt to put on a happy face, your young athletes will see through your façade and know how you really feel.

You must do everything you can to not feel or express negative emotions in your children's athletic lives. They will only make them feel bad. Ideally, having a healthy perspective will absolve you of any negative feelings that are often caused by a loss of perspective. But, in the real world, that's not always possible. In that case, I recommend that, if you can't let go of your negative emotions and generate genuine positive emotions when you're with your young athletes in a sports situation, you just stay away from them. Although they will certainly notice your absence, and perhaps even be disappointed by it, you will do far more harm than good if you stay around them when you're full of negativity.

> Anger doesn't solve anything. It builds nothing, but it can destroy everything. —*Lawrence Douglas Wilder, politician*[9]

Try to Motivate Your Children with Guilt

As a sport parent, you probably commit significant amounts of time, energy, and money to the pursuit of your children's athletic dreams. Although you likely do it willingly, if reluctantly, you may, nonetheless, feel some bitterness and resentment at the opportunity costs that are incurred. Those negative feelings can seep out of you, despite your best efforts, and tarnish your children's sports experiences.

A not uncommon refrain I hear from sport parents to their children is, "After all I do for you . . ." While intended to motivate young athletes, what it does mostly is cause your children to feel guilty about the time, energy, and money you're spending and the sacrifices you're making for their sports involvement. Yet, guilt is an unhealthy emotion to provoke in your children. It makes them feel really bad. It causes them to feel pressure to perform. And it leads them to resent you for putting that guilt on them.

If you feel angry, bitter, or resentful about your investment in your children's athletic lives, that is your problem, not theirs. You need to come to terms with it and not place that burden on their shoulders. You need to determine the investment you want to make and accept it. If you can't, get out of the sport. Of course, you want your children to fully appreciate and take advantage of the opportunities you are giving them. So, for example, if they're not working hard or taking care of their equipment, you need to have a talk with them, and a discussion of those costs and sacrifices might be appropriate. But it's best not to play the "Do you know how expensive your sport is?" guilt card to motivate your children. Instead, focus on why they aren't doing their job. Perhaps your children just don't enjoy it any longer and want to do something else, in which case you'll save yourself a lot of aggravation and money.

Look for a Financial ROI

I've already shared with you that looking for a financial return on investment (ROI) from your children's sports participation will result in a near-certain failure for both you and them. For every Simone Biles and Jordan Spieth you see at the top, there are thousands of athletes who dreamed big but didn't have what it took to climb to the pinnacle of their sport. And don't even think that a college scholarship will be a likely ROI; there are few of them, and they rarely cover the full cost of college. You'd be better off putting that money you spend on your children's sports in a 529 account. Of course, then your kids would miss out on a lot of fun and the wonderful benefits of sports involvement.

Live out Your Own Dreams in Your Children

In this aspirational culture in which we live, it's easy to be seduced by that pot of gold at the end of the rainbow. It is especially easy when you have unfulfilled dreams of your own as an athlete. I urge you not to live out your own dreams through your children's athletic pursuits. It's just not their job to fulfill your lost dreams as an athlete. Simply put, you should have your own dreams, and your children should have theirs and they shouldn't mix. Asking your children to live your dream will not only not fulfill your dream but also certainly turn their sports experiences into a nightmare.

Compare Your Children's Progress with Others

Where your young athletes finish when they are young or in comparison to others, as I note earlier in *Raising Young Athletes*, says little about where they will be in five or 10 years. Stars at age 12 are often not even in their sport any longer at age 15. Plus, neither you nor they have any control of other athletes. So, don't compare your children with other children in their sport. It in no way helps their progress and only makes them feel bad because they will feel incapable and unsupported. What matters is whether your children are progressing toward their goals. If you focus on that, they'll get as far as they can.

> Comparison is the thief of joy.
> —*Theodore Roosevelt, 26th president of the United States*[10]

Negatively Motivate

It can be frustrating when your young athletes aren't working as hard they can. You can feel downright angry as well. In this heightened negative emotional state, you look for ways to motivate them. Instead of stepping back from your ill feelings and looking closely and dispassionately at why they're not putting in their best effort and finding a solution, you will more likely just react and attempt to use some sort of force to motivate them. To that end, you may try to badger, harass, use sarcasm, threaten, pressure, or use fear to motivate your children. Admittedly, you may get results out of them for a while because fear can be a powerful motivator. But, at some point, they'll push back against your harsh tactics, and it won't be pretty. They will probably either sabotage their sports efforts or even quit to get back at you. Even worse, your punitive attempts at motivating them will cause real damage to your relationship with them, which could be permanent. And such severe methods only make you look like a bad parent, demean your children, and cause them to distance themselves from you.

> Don't force your kids into sports. I never was. To this day, my dad has never asked me to go play golf. I ask him. It's the child's desire to play that matters, not the parent's desire to have the child play.
> —*Tiger Woods, winner of 14 golf majors*[11]

Expect Results

As touched on earlier in *Raising Young Athletes*, expectations related to results are a burden that can crush young athletes' spirits and dreams. You should stay away from these outcome expectations at all costs. Don't ever expect anything of your children in their athletic lives other than their best effort and best behavior. Both of these expectations have several important benefits. Because effort is within their control, if they choose to give their best effort, they are likely to perform well, which will increase their chances of achieving their athletic goals. If they behave in ways that reflect healthy values, for example, being a good teammate, playing by the rules, taking responsibility, and being a gracious winner and loser, they are using sports to practice and more deeply ingrain those values, which will help them find happiness, satisfaction, and success both in their future athletic lives and beyond the field of play.

A message I try to convey throughout *Raising Young Athletes* is that success in sports should be defined far beyond victories, medals, and rankings. As you either approach or continue on your children's journey into the world of youth sports, you can have several other expectations for your children, including fun, an appreciation for physical health and fitness, mastery and love of sports, and, of course, those essential life lessons and tools they can use in all aspects of their lives moving forward.

Do Harm

Your children's sports participation should be a source of challenge, growth, pride, and inspiration for both you and your children. It should be an activity from which you and your children derive fun, joy, excitement, and fulfillment. It should never be an

> Your child's success or lack of success in sports does not indicate the kind of parent you are. But having an athlete that is coachable, respectful, a great teammate, mentally tough, resilient, and tries their best *is* a direct reflection of your parenting. —*Bruce Brown, founder of Proactive Coaching*[12]

experience that hurts you or your children, whether physically, psychologically, emotionally, or socially. So, to conclude *Raising Young Athletes*, and I write this capitalized to ensure that you get this final message loud and clear: DON'T EVER DO ANYTHING THAT WILL CAUSE YOUR YOUNG ATHLETES TO THINK LESS OF THEMSELVES OR YOU!!!

EPILOGUE

To be the best sport parent you can be. To raise young athletes who are determined, confident, and resilient both within and outside of their sports lives. Admirable goals, to be sure. And equally difficult to achieve. In a day and age when everything is supposed to be easier, being a parent, much less a sport parent, is decidedly not.

You certainly face a strong headwind as you pursue these goals in the form of a youth sports culture that has lost its way, no longer focuses on the needs of young athletes, and communicates many unhealthy messages to your children in their athletic lives. You must face your children's own inertia, which impels them to take the path of least resistance in many aspects of their lives. Lastly, you may have to confront the biggest obstacle to those goals—yourself. You may have your own baggage about sports from your own athletic experiences when you were young. You are also vulnerable to the seductive messages from the youth sports culture about fame and future for your young athletes. And you now may have an overly scheduled life where it feels as if you can barely get through the day meeting your children's needs, much less your own, and simply don't have the time or energy to focus on goals that you know are important to your children in their athletic lives.

Because of this challenge, which is both internal and external, I have come to believe that courage, commitment, and persistence are the three most important qualities you need to raise successful and happy athletes and young people. You need the courage to confront a powerful and oftentimes malevolent youth sports culture and the forces within you that may make you susceptible to its unhealthy messages. You must have the strength to acknowledge those forces and resist them with all your might. You must have the mettle to make the right choice with every decision, as it could either help or hurt your children's efforts as they pursue their athletic goals.

You must also commit to doing the right thing for your young athletes not only as an idea or theory, but in the always busy and sometimes chaotic daily experiences of your family's lives. This commitment will help you see that every one of these experiences is an opportunity to shape your children as you know they should be or as our youth sports culture wants them to be. Commitment ensures that you make the right choice every day to have a positive impact on your children in their athletic lives and beyond.

You must acknowledge that the road to raising successful and happy young athletes will be bumpy with many obstacles and setbacks. As such, you need to be persistent in your efforts to not only do the right thing for your children but also resist the forces, both local and cultural, that want to pull you and them onto an entirely different road.

If you stay on the good road as you and your children navigate their athletic lives, you may not fully appreciate the wonderful lifelong gifts that you give your children within or outside of sports. You may not even notice the gifts because they will be so embedded in your children and so consistent with the values, attitudes, and practices in which you immersed them. What the gifts provide are not just about what you see in your children: determination, confidence, focus, resilience, and so much more. It also involves what you won't see: ego, selfishness, disrespect. Your children may not even be aware of these gifts as they're growing up because the gifts have been so woven into your family, who they are, and the way they lead their lives as athletes and people. But those gifts will always be there and guide their lives as surely as road signs direct drivers to their destination.

I hope that *Raising Young Athletes* has provided you with the knowledge, insights, and tools to help you become the best sport parent you can be and help your children become successful and happy athletes and young people. But the responsibility to use the information is yours. You are now faced with a fork in the road that will impact you and your children both within and outside their athletic lives for their entire lives.

Which road do you choose?

NOTES

INTRODUCTION

1. Douglas Brunt, "Money Has Ruined Youth Sports," *Time*, May 3, 2017. Accessed June 9, 2017, http://time.com/4757448/youth-sports-pay/.

2. Greg Bach, "Prominent Surgeon's Insight Youth Sports Parents Can't Ignore," *Sporting Kid Live*, May 12, 2017. Accessed June 9, 2017, http://nays.org/sklive/features /prominent-surgeon-s-insight-youth-sports-parents-can-t-ignore/?platform=hootsuite.

3. NAYS.org, "@OSUCoachSchiano: 'In #youthsports No One Is Losing Their Job on the Win or Loss So Let's Make Sure That the Kids Are Coming Back to Play,'" *Twitter*, November 30, 2016. Accessed June 10, 2017, https://twitter.com/NAYS_edu /status/804008412409434112.

4. NAYS.org, "@Orioles Showalter: 'You're Not Developing People for the Next Level, You're Developing People for the Next Level of Life.'" *Twitter*, May 26, 2017. Accessed June 10, 2017, https://twitter.com/NAYS_edu/status/868246642302087169 /photo/1.

5. Janis B. Meredith, *11 Habits of Happy and Positive Sports Parents* (Place of Publication Not Identified: BookBaby, 2016).

CHAPTER 1

1. "Madhuri Dixit Quote," *BrainyQuote*, 2017. Accessed July 28, 2017, https:// www.brainyquote.com/quotes/quotes/m/madhuridix623645.html.

2. "Cal Ripken Jr. Quote," *Pinterest*, 2017. Accessed November 15, 2017, https:// www.pinterest.com/pin/553872454146516881.

3. "Frank Sonnenberg Quote," *Pinterest*, 2017. Accessed November 15, 2017, https://www.pinterest.com/myenglishteache/english-quotes/?lp=true.

4. "Chris Evert Quote," *BrainyQuote*, 2017. Accessed November 15, 2017, https://www.brainyquote.com/quotes/quotes/c/chrisevert181271.html.

5. Andy Smithson, "Meet the Family," *Truparenting.net*, 2017. Accessed July 28, 2017, http://truparenting.net/about/the-smithson-family/.

6. "Why J. J. Watt Doesn't Want You to Play Just One Sport," *Stack.com*, 2017. Accessed October 31, 2017, http://www.stack.com/a/why-j-j-watt-doesnt-want-you-to-play-just-one-sport.

7. "Steve Jobs Quote," *Goodreads.com*, 2017. Accessed October 31, 2017, https://www.goodreads.com/quotes/445287-don-t-let-the-noise-of-others-opinions-drown-out-your.

8. Pam Leo, "Connection Parenting and Optimal Child Development," *Connectionparenting.com*, 2017. Accessed November 4, 2017, http://www.connectionparenting.com/parenting_articles/index.html.

9. "Louise Hart Quotes," *Drlouisehart.com*, 2017. Accessed November 7, 2017, https://drlouisehart.com/about/quotes/.

10. "LeBron James Quotes," *BrainyQuote*, 2017. Accessed August 11, 2017, https://www.brainyquote.com/quotes/quotes/l/lebronjame425370.html.

11. "Accountability Quotes, Derek Lauber," *Pinterest*, 2017. Accessed November 7, 2017, https://www.pinterest.com/explore/accountability-quotes/?lp=true.

12. "Wrestling Live," *Pinterest*, 2017. Accessed November 7, 2017, https://www.pinterest.com/explore/wrestling-live/?lp=true.

13. "Motivational Quotes," *Thewoodeneffect.com*, 2017. Accessed November 7, 2017, https://www.thewoodeneffect.com/motivational-quotes/.

CHAPTER 2

1. "Henry Ford Quote," *BrainyQuote*, 2017. Accessed November 13, 2017, https://www.brainyquote.com/topics/goal.

2. "The Best 550 Random Quotes, Life Advice, and Sayings," *Livelifehappy.com*, 2017. Accessed November 13, 2017, https://livelifehappy.com/random-life-quotes/.

3. "Fear of Failure Quotes," *Goodreads.com*, 2017. Accessed November 13, 2017, https://www.goodreads.com/author/quotes/5116439.L_R_Knost.

4. Marcy McKay, "The Top Three Fears Sabotaging Your Writing (and the Solutions)," *Positivewriter.com*, 2017. Accessed November 13, 2017, http://positivewriter.com/fears-writing-solutions/.

5. "Fear of Failure Quotes," *Goodreads.com*, 2017. Accessed November 13, 2017, https://www.goodreads.com/quotes/tag/fear-of-failure.

6. "Quotes to Overcome Fear of Failure," *Calebwojcik.com*, 2017. Accessed November 13, 2017, http://www.calebwojcik.com/blog/2012/01/30/quotes-overcome-fear-of-failure.

7. "Michael Jordan Quote," *BrainyQuote*, 2017. Accessed August 18, 2017, https://www.brainyquote.com/quotes/quotes/m/michaeljor447196.html.

8. "Failure-Motivation Quotes," *Pinterest*, 2017. Accessed November 13, 2017, https://www.pinterest.com/explore/failure-quotes-motivation/?lp=true.

9. "Sport Psychology Quotes," *Sportpsychquotes.wordpress.com*, 2017. Accessed November 13, 2017, https://sportpsychquotes.wordpress.com/tag/emotionsfeelings/.

10. "Sport Psychology Quotes," *Sportpsychquotes.wordpress.com*, 2017. Accessed November 13, 2017, https://sportpsychquotes.wordpress.com/tag/emotionsfeelings/.

11. "Bob Keeshan Quote," *BrainyQuote*, 2017. Accessed November 13, 2017, https://www.brainyquote.com/topics/role_models.

12. "Emotional Intelligence," *Trans4mind.com*, 2017. Accessed November 13, 2017, https://trans4mind.com/quotes/quotes-emotional-intelligence.html.

13. "High Expectations Quotes," *Pinterest*, 2017. Accessed November 13, 2017, https://www.pinterest.com/explore/high-expectations-quotes/?lp=true.

14. "Life Coaching," *Understandingrelationships.com*, 2017. Accessed November 13, 2017, https://understandingrelationships.com/life-coaching-services/.

15. "Best Love Quotes and Life Quotes," *Purehappylife.com*, 2017. Accessed November 13, 2017, http://purehappylife.com/?s=fall+in+love+with+the+process&submit=Search.

16. "Funny Quotes and Sayings," *Pinterest*, 2017. Accessed November 13, 2017, https://www.pinterest.com/nacrowther/funny-quotes-and-sayings/?lp=true.

CHAPTER 3

1. "Happiness Quotes," *Pinterest*, 2017. Accessed November 14, 2017, https://www.pinterest.com/pin/497929302526234930/?lp=true.

2. Greg Bach, "Tampa Bay Great Hardy Nickerson Talks Coaching Kids," *NAYS.org*, October 9, 2015. Accessed September 26, 2017, http://www.nays.org/sklive/features/all-pro-coaching-advice-rev-up-your-excitement-level-at-practice/.

3. "Happiness Quotes," *Pinterest*, 2017. Accessed November 14, 2017, https://www.pinterest.com/pin/412149803370887265/.

4. "We Are One Team," *Abettermedaybyday.com*, 2017. Accessed November 14, 2017, https://www.google.com/search?q=abettermedaybyday&tbm=isch&tbo=u&source=univ&sa=X&ved=0ahUKEwiTkobY377XAhUT1WMKHem1CKIQsAQIJw&biw=1366&bih=647.

5. "Sixty-Six Inspiring Olympics Quotes from Players and Coaches," *Thefreshquotes.com*, 2017. Accessed November 14, 2017, https://www.thefreshquotes.com/66-inspiring-olympics-quotes-from-players-coaches/.

6. "Misty May-Treanor Quote," *BrainyQuote*, 2017. Accessed September 27, 2017, https://www.brainyquote.com/authors/misty_maytreanor.

7. "Brene Brown Quote," *Quotefancy*, 2017. Accessed November 14, 2017, https://quotefancy.com/quote/777727/Bren-Brown-We-re-a-nation-of-exhausted-and -over-stressed-adults-raising-over-scheduled.

8. "American Football Quotes: Vince Lombardi," *Quotesta.com*, 2017. Accessed November 14, 2017, http://quotesta.com/category/sports-quotes/page/2/.

9. "Goal-Setting Quotes," *Pinterest*, 2017. Accessed November 14, 2017, https://www.pinterest.com/explore/goal-setting-quotes/?lp=true.

10. "Parenting Quotes," *Pinterest*, 2017. Accessed November 14, 2017, https://www.pinterest.com/kajutime/parenting-quotes/?lp=true.

11. "Raising a Child Quotes," *Pinterest*, 2017. Accessed November 14, 2017, https://www.pinterest.com/pin/631770653947023638/?lp=true.

CHAPTER 4

1. "Sports Parents," *Pinterest*, 2017. Accessed November 15, 2017, https://www.pinterest.com/luckywoyak/sports-parents/?lp=true.

2. "Don Shula Quote," *BrainyQuote*, 2017. Accessed November 15, 2017, https://www.brainyquote.com/quotes/quotes/d/donshula155889.html.

3. "Bode Miller Quote," *IzQuotes*, 2017. Accessed September 27, 2017, http://izquotes.com/quote/253070.

4. "Charles Barkley Quote," *IzQuotes*, 2017. Accessed November 15, 2017, http://izquotes.com/quote/298399.

5. "Sports Parents," *Pinterest*, 2017. Accessed November 15, 2017, https://www.pinterest.com/luckywoyak/sports-parents/?lp=true.

6. "Bob Talbert Quote," *Upward.org*, 2017. Accessed November 15, 2017, http://www.upward.org/blog.

7. "Michael Lewis Quote," *IzQuotes*, 2017. Accessed November 15, 2017, http://izquotes.com/quote/111840.

8. "Muhammad Ali Quote," *BrainyQuote*, 2017. Accessed November 15, 2017, https://www.brainyquote.com/quotes/quotes/m/muhammadal120238.html.

CHAPTER 5

1. "MOTA Quotes: Parents, Coaches, and Fans," *Pinterest*, 2017. Accessed November 16, 2017, https://www.pinterest.com/mindotathlete/mota-quotes-parents -coaches-and-fans/.

2. "Bob Bigelow Quotes," *QuoteHD.com*, 2017. Accessed November 15, 2017, http://www.quotehd.com/quotes/bob-bigelow-quote-i-really-got-into-this-after-seeing -a-series-of-negative-events.

3. "Elizabeth Andrews Quote," *Pinterest*, 2017. Accessed November 16, 2017, https://www.pinterest.com/pin/72972456439771053/?lp=true.

4. "Baseball Signs," *Pinterest*, 2017. Accessed November 16, 2017, https://www.pinterest.com/pin/357473289154193581/.

5. "Great Coaches Thank You Quotes," *QuotesGram*, 2017. Accessed November 16, 2017, http://quotesgram.com/great-coaches-thank-you-quotes/.

6. "Football Quotes/Motivation," *Pinterest*, 2017. Accessed November 16, 2017, https://www.pinterest.com/raysiii/football-quotes-motivation/.

7. "Kids Humor," *Pinterest*, 2017. Accessed November 16, 2017, https://www.pinterest.com/alenachka999/kids-humor/.

8. Jamie McKinven, "Ten Sanity Tips for Minor Parents," *Glassandout.com*. 2017. Accessed November 16, 2017, https://glassandout.com/2014/02/10-sanity-tips-for-minor-hockey-parents/.

9. "Anger Resources for Parents," *Toddlerapproved.com*, 2017. Accessed November 16, 2017, http://www.toddlerapproved.com/2014/09/anger-resources-for-parents.html.

10. "Theodore Roosevelt Quote," *Quotefancy*, 2017. Accessed November 17, 2017, https://quotefancy.com/quote/33048/Theodore-Roosevelt-Comparison-is-the-thief-of-joy.

11. "Tiger Woods Quote," *IzQuotes*, 2017. Accessed November 15, 2017, http://izquotes.com/quote/201571.

12. John O'Sullivan, "Parental Athletic Dreams Can Become Youth Sports Nightmares," *Huffingtonpost.com*, March 11, 2015. Accessed November 17, 2017, https://www.huffingtonpost.com/john-oasullivan/parental-athletic-dreams-_b_6850790.html.

BIBLIOGRAPHY

Bach, Greg. "Prominent Surgeon's Insight Youth Sports Parents Can't Ignore." *Sporting Kid Live*, May 12, 2017. Accessed June 9, 2017, http://nays.org/sklive/features/prominent -surgeon-s-insight-youth-sports-parents-can-t-ignore/?platform=hootsuite.

——. "Tampa Bay Great Hardy Nickerson Talks Coaching Kids." *NAYS.org*, October 9, 2015. Accessed September 26, 2017, http://www.nays.org/sklive/features/all- pro-coaching-advice-rev-up-your-excitement-level-at-practice/.

Battles, Ryan. "Comparison Is the Thief of Joy." *RyanBattles.com*, 2017. Accessed October 6, 2017, https://ryanbattles.com/post/comparison-is-the-thief-of-joy.

Brewer, Britton W., Judy L. Van Raalte, and Darwyn E. Linder. "Athletic Identity: Hercules' Muscles or Achilles Heel?" *International Journal of Sport Psychology* 24, no. 2 (1993): 237–54.

Brunt, Douglas. "Money Has Ruined Youth Sports." *Time*, May 3, 2017. Accessed June 9, 2017, http://time.com/4757448/youth-sports-pay/.

Cesare, Nick, Sarah Landrum, and Karen Kolp, et al. "20 Inspirational Quotes for Kids to Inspire Their Best." *Everyday Power Blog*, 2014. Accessed October 6, 2017, https://everydaypowerblog.com/2014/05/25/motivational-quotes-for-kids/.

Fendrich, Howard. "7-Foot-9 Player Joins ABA Club." *Associated Press*, January 31, 2007. Accessed March 19, 2007, http://www.washingtonpost.com/wp-dyn/content /article/2007/01/31/AR2007013101778_pf.html.

"Fifty-Five Most Famous Inspirational Sports Quotes of All-Time." *BrightDrops. com*, 2016. Accessed October 6, 2017, http://brightdrops.com/inspirational-sports -quotes.

Ginsburg, Richard D., Steven R. Smith, Nicole Danforth, T. Atilla Ceranoglu, Stephen A. Durant, Hayley Kamin, Rebecca Babcock, Lucy Robin, and Bruce Masek. "Patterns of Specialization in Professional Baseball Players." *Journal of Clinical Sport Psychology* 8, no. 3 (2014): 261–75.

"Have Any MLB Players Played in the LLWS???" *Answers.Yahoo.com*, 2017. Accessed November 15, 2017, https://answers.yahoo.com/question/index?qid=20070823200 950AA0Okao.

Jayanthi, Neeru A., Cynthia R. LaBella, Daniel Fischer, Jacqueline Pasulka, and Lara R. Dugas. "Sports-Specialized Intensive Training and the Risk of Injury in Young Athletes: A Clinical Case-Control Study." *American Journal of Sports Medicine* 43, no. 4 (2015): 794–801.

Meredith, Janis B. *11 Habits of Happy and Positive Sports Parents*. Place of Publication Not Identified: BookBaby, 2016.

Michael, Jonathan. "Pause: 10 Quotes on Why You Should Take Breaks, Relax, and Play." *Bplans Blog*, 2016. Accessed October 6, 2017, http://articles.bplans.com /pause-quotes-take-breaks-relax-play/.

NAYS.org. "@Orioles Showalter: 'You're Not Developing People for the Next Level, You're Developing People for the Next Level of Life.'" *Twitter*, May 26, 2017. Accessed June 10, 2017, https://twitter.com/NAYS_edu/status/868246642302087169/ photo/1.

——. "@OSUCoachSchiano: 'In #youthsports No One Is Losing Their Job on the Win or Loss So Let's Make Sure That the Kids Are Coming Back to Play.'" *Twitter*, November 30, 2016. Accessed June 10, 2017, https://twitter.com/NAYS_edu /status/804008412409434112.

O'Sullivan, John. "Parental Athletic Dreams Can Become Youth Sports Nightmares." *Huffingtonpost.com*, March 11, 2015. Accessed November 17, 2017, https://www .huffingtonpost.com/john-oasullivan/parental-athletic-dreams-_b_6850790.html.

"Pope Francis Quotes." *BrainyQuote*, 2017. Accessed October 6, 2017, https://www .brainyquote.com/quotes/quotes/p/popefranci521189.html.

"Quotes about Sport Participation (12 Quotes)." *Quotemaster.org*, 2017. Accessed October 6, 2017, http://www.quotemaster.org/sport+participation.

"Results from the 2015 GOALS Study of the Student-Athlete Experience." NCAA Convention, January 2016. *NCAA.org*. Accessed November 15, 2017, https://www .ncaa.org/sites/default/files/GOALS_convention_slidebank_jan2016_public.pdf.

Roskvist, Katie. "Coaching Quotes from the Best Sports Coaches." *Athlete Assessments*, 2014. Accessed October 6, 2017, http://athleteassessments.com/coaching-quotes-best-sports-coaches/.

"Sports Parenting: Get the Most Out of Your Child's Sports Experience." *Sports Parenting Podcast/JBM Thinks*, 2017. Accessed November 15, 2017, https://jbmthinks .com/sports-parenting-youth-sports/.

Vidic, Zachary. "A Phenomenological Study: The Experience of Parenting an Elite Youth Athlete." Master's thesis, Barry University, 2016.

Wallace, Jennifer B. "Why Kids Shouldn't Specialize in One Sport." *Huffingtonpost.com*, August 18, 2015. Accessed November 15, 2017, https://www.huffingtonpost.com /jennifer-breheny-wallace/why-kids-shouldnt-specialize-in-one-sport_b_7972286. html.

ABOUT THE AUTHOR

Jim Taylor is an internationally recognized authority on the psychology of sport and parenting. He has consulted with athletes, coaches, and parents for more than 30 years. Dr. Taylor has worked with professional, Olympic, collegiate, and junior-elite athletes in football, baseball, basketball, lacrosse, swimming, tennis, golf, ski racing, and many other sports.

Taylor received his bachelor's degree from Middlebury College and earned his master's degree and Ph.D. in psychology from the University of Colorado. He was an associate professor in the School of Psychology at Nova University in Ft. Lauderdale, a clinical associate professor in the master's in sport and performance psychology program at the University of Denver, and is currently an adjunct professor in the sports management program at the University of San Francisco.

Taylor is the author of 16 books, including eight sport psychology books and five parenting books. He is also the editor of three textbooks related to sport psychology. He has published more than 600 articles in popular and professional publications, and given more than 1,000 workshops and presentations throughout North America and Europe. Taylor's blog posts have been read by more than 10 million people on www.psychologytoday.com and www.huffingtonpost.com, as well as on his own website. He also publishes two widely read e-newsletters, "Prime Sport Alert!" and "Prime Family Alert!"

A former internationally ranked alpine ski racer, Taylor is a certified tennis coach, a second-degree black belt, a certified instructor in karate, a marathon runner, and an Ironman triathlete.

He lives north of San Francisco with his wife and two daughters, both of whom are competitive athletes.

To learn more, visit www.drjimtaylor.com.